Discoveries Through Personal Agility

Discoveries Through Personal Agility

Raji Sivaraman
Michal Raczka

BEP
BUSINESS EXPERT PRESS
Leader in applied, concise business books

First published in 2020 by
Business Expert Press, LLC
222 East 46th Street, New York, NY 10017
www.businessexpertpress.com

ISBN-13: 978-1-95253-802-5 (paperback)
ISBN-13: 978-1-95253-803-2 (e-book)

Business Expert Press Portfolio and Project Management Collection

Collection ISSN: 2156-8189 (print)
Collection ISSN: 2156-8200 (electronic)

Cover and interior design by S4Carlisle Publishing Services Private Ltd., Chennai, India

First edition: 2020

10 9 8 7 6 5 4 3 2 1

Printed in the United States of America.

Abstract

This book explores the nuances of different aspects of agility on a personal level. Agility brings personal value, leadership navigation, managing the tides of knowledge, and putting on the captain's hat of resilience. As the winds change and the tides swell high, the Personal Agility Lighthouse (PALH™) model in this book will guide you to safe shores. Navigating through the seven colors of agility such as education, change, emotional, political, cerebral, learning, and outcomes agilities, the anchor is dropped effortlessly. It is built on these seven competencies, and by using the Individual Personal Agility self-analysis assessment (see Appendix), swaying personal visions leading them up to organizational goals.

Taking personal agility as the future competency with an agile mindset is a crucial starting point to transform yourself. Focusing your personal agility journey on outcomes and end-to-end customer experiences ensures value delivery. Especially within the elements of the VUCA environment where revised goals are the norm. Driving changes in the right direction leads you to the stable grounds of your personal vision. It prepares you to tread the long roads of transitions/transformations, which is a vital requisite for changes in any organization. Measuring performance metrics aptly is the rudder of strategy management and stability.

Organizational goals and personal development are the strong pillars that will steer you to your organizational agility, getting you ready for opportunities and changes when your company trademark needs it. Agile practices and perspectives cut through impact and quality of personal and group knowledge. Take a journey on a Personal Agility Boat to visualize options, alternatives, and opportunities. Visualization is the way to your shore's lighthouse.

Keywords

personal agility; stable adaptability; innovative thinking; agile mindset; empathy; future competency; re-skilling; organizational transformation

Contents

Preface

In this book, we are going to describe how we embarked on a model for honing Personal Agility. It details the nuances of how the agile mindset of an individual transcends all the way from Personal Agility to Organizational Agility. We probe into how the behavior and understanding of the agile mindsets and various agility flavors are directly proportional to the disruptive business world we live in today.

A Singapore citizen Raji Sivaraman meets a Polish citizen Michal Raczka at a conference and the chat takes its turn toward the "agile mindset." All of the problems we faced in the tech, project management, supply chain, logistics, and a number of other fields world seem to stem from one cause, which is the way people's mind is set. This then brought us to think about what we can do to change mindsets and why we need to do this. We pondered, researched, and read about many agile theories, looked for answers by talking, interviewing, and asking academia folks their take on this. Everywhere and anyone we interacted with, within and outside of our work and academia world, there were seven agilities that came to the forefront all the time. They are Education Agility, Change Agility, Political Agility, Emotional Agility, Cerebral Agility, Learning Agility, and Outcomes agility.

Since we were repeatedly hearing the same seven agilities come up over and over again, we figured these must be the most important to hone personal agility within an individual and an organization. In our minds, a project is all about the complexities in today's fast-paced, competitive, and dynamic environment. It does not matter what kind of projects we plunge into. It could be any industry: small, medium, large, or mega. Besides there are a lot of ambiguity, we need to deal with human behaviors. From our perspective, personal agility with its seven flavors can positively influence the ability to manage complexities and this can be considered as an ultimate goal to deliver the expected projects' and organizational outcomes.

We decided to write research and academic papers and papers for conferences where we could validate the need and the importance of the seven agilities that we found quintessential. We asked organizations to use it and they have written articles from different countries (such as Poland, Indonesia, the United States of America, the United Kingdom, to name a few). They were from different industries as well, for example, Palm Oil, Academia, Consulting, etc. Articles were written about the use of this model on varied subjects like portfolio management, data analytics, and green effort as samples. Some of these examples are quoted in this book. This encouraged us to reaffirm that these are the seven that we should add to our model. The reasons are because these were the seven that almost all of them found a need to hone in their work and academic space at all levels.

Many believed that personal agility is too advanced for practitioners to absorb as of today. Leadership skills and its talks and theories have been around for many years, but when it comes to personal agility, it is still a new concept. People mix up the theories and what leadership skills and personal agility skills are all about. Leadership is about leading and making sure that everything goes well whether there is a change or not. Whereas personal agility talks about how one can ride the waves of change specifically. Some people said that agile cannot be soft. To them we said, Agile is about the thought process and the tools, processes, and methodologies are about how you do manage and deliver projects and ultimately the organization.

All of these questions prompted us to come up with the self-analysis, which we normally give at the beginning of the Personal Agility workshop. This is where the message got across in a solid way. It showed whether personal agility can make you more agile. Once the participants in workshops took the self-analysis, they started to understand what agilities they needed to hone. They themselves started telling us that personal agility makes them more agile. Finally, we decided on the name of our model as the Personal Agility Lighthouse model because of what a lighthouse stands for and its symbolism to our topic: personal agility became more and more synonymous. This is explained in our introduction.

Let's set sail!!

Introduction

From an organization's perspective, personal agility is very important especially in this current era where business is changing at a very fast pace. There are many seminars, workshops, and exams for tools and methodologies in every organization. There are various models to develop people in a collective setting. Nevertheless, when it comes to the agility at a personal level, not much is out there to address in this arena. Therefore, to enhance the business agility in any given company, institution, or entity, an individual's agility in many facets needs attention and honing.

"Enterprises must embrace a more fluid way of working to compete effectively—one that quickly allows for new technologies to be assessed, tested, analyzed, and acted upon. This 'fail fast, succeed faster' mentality requires a fundamental shift in work culture and behavior."[1]

"Strive for progress not perfection" (unknown)

This quote personifies the Personal Agility Lighthouse (PALH™) model[2] shown below in Figure 1 wholistically. This is one of the reasons we refer to the lighthouse as the goal. What does a lighthouse stand for and its symbolism to our topic *Personal Agility*? Lighthouses are constructed to withstand powerful storms and are frequently depicted as symbols of strength. They are also used to symbolize shelter, protection, and peace for the same reason. Lighthouses expose the connection between inanimate structures and human emotion in a way that few other buildings can. Equipped with powerful radio transmitters and lights bright enough to penetrate the darkness, lighthouses serve as maritime and aerial navigational aids. They are often used to symbolize true guidance and steadfastness in relationships, teams, and organizations, encapsulating their ability to weather any storm. Lighthouses have also been used to represent the determination to achieve goals, no matter the challenges. They are almost always erected in desolate places because that is where the guidance is of utmost importance. That is the symbolism that the seven agilities hold where individuals and teams hone their *personal agility* to achieve project and organizational performance excellence.

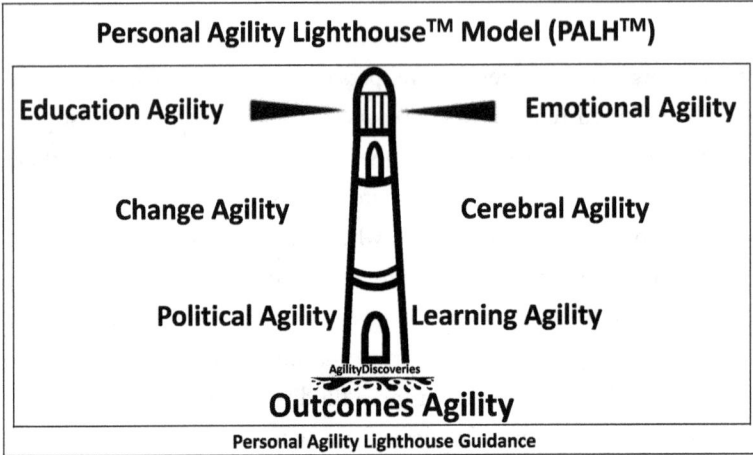

Personal Agility Lighthouse™ Model (PALH™)

Education Agility ▶◀ Emotional Agility

Change Agility   Cerebral Agility

Political Agility   Learning Agility

AgilityDiscoveries

Outcomes Agility

Personal Agility Lighthouse Guidance

Raji Sivaraman & Michal Raczka 2017

Figure 1

A lighthouse's strong design and aura of imperturbability are used to depict strength and virility to withstand the strongest storms. However, lighthouses do not always evoke positive feelings. Because lighthouses tend to be located in isolated areas, they can symbolize fear, desolation, and death. Additionally, since their blinding light has occasionally guided ships to their destruction, lighthouses can represent deception and betrayal. Escape from inside a lighthouse is virtually impossible; for this reason, they have also been employed as symbols of bondage. *Personal agility* is no different with its ups and downs. Finding a way through these travails is what the seven agilities are deployed for.

The preamble to implement the model is to have an agile mindset. The framework will work only if the conviction is attuned to this outlook. The skill sets needed to tackle tomorrow's possibilities is by charting a plan for self-improvement in our minds. The solutions for the challenges of tomorrow has its foundations in the experiences of today. We plan, sell, communicate, collaborate, and network globally across all cultures. We must embark on an honest reflection of what we do today and make conscious improvements. This process coupled with continuous learning will lead to the skill sets to break the paradigms and tackle the possibilities of the future.

To elaborate further; the VIBGYOR (Versatility, Ingenuity, Bridging, Gold Plating, Yield, Originality, Resilience)[3] concept where management is shown as pursuing behaviors of management in various disciplines that engages and develops originality and creativeness for exceedingly successful outcomes and performances. Here management can be seen as a multicolored rainbow, where Versatility is stated as dependencies that link the management chain without breakage, but at the same time these dependencies need a versatile approach for easy collaboration and execution. This concept holds water in the performance of teams where each of the seven agilities is to be groomed as well.

We feel it is important that high performance in an organization is imperative. Perspectives of these seven flavors of ours are the sails that need to be directed appropriately for an organization to have its performance at its peak in our minds. Indeed, the search for competitive advantage is driving much of the rapid development amidst various dimensions. By improving the decision-making capability of managers and teams, management can help an organization enhance its competitive position in the market and be a high performer with profitability hand in hand. McClelland[4] contended that three dominant needs underpin human motivation. The following three are the needs:

- **Needs for achievement**
- **Needs for power**
- **Needs for affiliation**

McClelland believed that the relative importance of each need varies among individuals and cultures. We feel that to understand this the seven agilities are to be embedded in the veins.

We take this theory a couple of steps further with the seven agilities of *education agility, change agility, emotional agility, political agility, cerebral agility, learning agility* and *outcomes agility* that we feel show the guiding light to the intended shore. High-performing organizations, those we call champions, develop the capability to continually finding your feet, adjusting, and innovating. To further this thought, Victor Vroom's Expectancy Theory[5] states that the intensity of a tendency to perform in a particular manner is dependent on the intensity of an expectation that the performance will be followed by a definite outcome and on the appeal of the outcome to the individual.

Discoveries through the journey of all the agilities brought us to the conclusion and research plus interviews unearthed that there is certainly a logic and segue so to speak for these seven agilities to have a distinct value chain. The value stream mapping is shown below.

Logic to the sequence for the seven agilities of the PALH^{TM} model to transform individuals

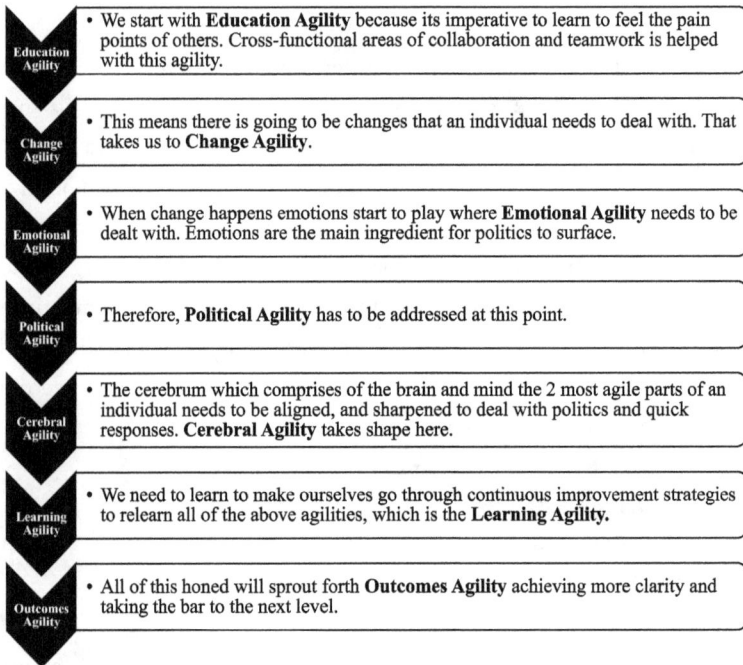

Education Agility	• We start with **Education Agility** because its imperative to learn to feel the pain points of others. Cross-functional areas of collaboration and teamwork is helped with this agility.
Change Agility	• This means there is going to be changes that an individual needs to deal with. That takes us to **Change Agility**.
Emotional Agility	• When change happens emotions start to play where **Emotional Agility** needs to be dealt with. Emotions are the main ingredient for politics to surface.
Political Agility	• Therefore, **Political Agility** has to be addressed at this point.
Cerebral Agility	• The cerebrum which comprises of the brain and mind the 2 most agile parts of an individual needs to be aligned, and sharpened to deal with politics and quick responses. **Cerebral Agility** takes shape here.
Learning Agility	• We need to learn to make ourselves go through continuous improvement strategies to relearn all of the above agilities, which is the **Learning Agility.**
Outcomes Agility	• All of this honed will sprout forth **Outcomes Agility** achieving more clarity and taking the bar to the next level.

The end goal is to get better at what you do, which can be enabled by ideation. According to Wikipedia, the word "Ideation"⁶ is the creative process of generating, developing, and communicating new ideas, where an idea is understood as a basic element of thought that can be visual, concrete, or abstract. Ideation comprises all stages of a thought cycle, from innovation, to development, to actualization.

"Ideate" is simply a tie into learning agility, education agility, and cerebral agility, which aligns with personal agility. Engaging these three supports the three concepts of personal agility, namely political agility, emotional agility, and change agility, making the ideation come to life. This brings about the perfect outcome intended, bringing the outcomes agility into the right beam of light. One needs to have change agility to ideate and engage.

As we go from personal agility, all the way to organizational agility, we sail through the seven principles given below that clear the path to the lighthouse. In the chapters that follow, we are going to elaborate the principles of our model given below.

Principles of the PALH™ model

1. We need to constantly keep advancing ourselves to reroute our capabilities—**Education Agility**
2. We need to relearn ourselves to improve competencies—**Change Agility**
3. We have to treat others with deference—**Emotional Agility**
4. We need transparency for organizational growth—**Political Agility**
5. We need to focus on organizational goals not the impediments of alterations—**Cerebral Agility**
6. We need to have the courage to say "I don't know"—**Learning Agility**
7. We need to commit to excel in the outcome that is foreseen—**Outcomes Agility**

Acknowledgments

We would like to acknowledge the support of our publishers, Business Expert Press.

We are deeply grateful to Ricardo Viana Vargas and Robin Speculand for writing the forewords for us.

We would like to thank IRIS for their partnership, in particular Douglas Heikkinen, Cofounder, Publisher, and Editor of IRIS, USA for publishing the articles written by many of the international experts. We express our immense gratitude to all of them. We thank Marguerita Cheng, CEO of Blue Ocean Global Wealth, Washington D.C., USA, for introducing us to IRIS and contributing to the subject as well.

The following contributors have also been quoted in this book.

Thomas Martin, CEO, Forward Intelligence Group, Singapore/ Philippines/Germany

Patrick N Connally, Director, Teradata, Philadelphia, USA

Professor Linh Luong, Program Director of M.S. in Project Management, University of Seattle

Rafael De La Rosa, Project-Portfolio Management Consultant, Indonesia/ Spain

Paul Hodgkins, Executive Director, Paul Hodgkins Project Consultancy, United Kingdom

Makheni Zonneveld, Future Readiness Coach, the Netherlands

Joanna Staniszewska CEO, You'll Ltd., Poland

Gaurav Dhooper, Program Manager, RPA & Agile Practitioner at Genpact, India

We would like to thank Brian Richard for the long hours spent in conceptually and logically designing the front cover.

Last, but not least, we would like to thank our colleagues, families, and friends for giving us the time and space to do the research and put in the hours of dedicated stretches to get our book on its final sail.

Foreword

By
Robin Speculand
*Author of Excellence in Execution and Digital
Implementation Specialist*

An expression that has become very common is that today's leader requires a digital mindset. But what does that mean? It means they need to recognize that the way they conducted business yesterday no longer guarantees results tomorrow. It means letting go of power to empower employees to make rapid decisions as they participate in different events such as hackathons, design thinking and customer journeys. It means dramatically reducing the bureaucracy in the organization while eliminating silo mentality and it also means being personally agile.

Raji and Michal beautifully explain what this means and demonstrate how leaders can achieve this by adopting the ***Personal Agility Lighthouse (PALH™) model.***

Implementation for organizations is becoming tougher with my own research revealing that over two-thirds fail. Adopting digitalization fails even more - 80 per cent of the time, according to various research. A key reason for the high failure rate is that leaders require a different mind and skill set to lead today's organization. By being personally agile leaders are more conscious of the shifting strategic landscape, quicker to respond to customer and market requirements and more open to transforming their leadership style to lead in this new way of conducting business. But this is not easy to achieve. My 2019 research revealed that one of the top three reasons organizations fail to adopt digitalization is because of – leaders' mindset.

Raji and Michal address this head on and explain how leaders can achieve high performance in this turbulent time. In organization agility, customer pain points are identified. In personal agility leaders identify their employee pain points and rectify them and the Personal Agility Lighthouse (PALH™) model provides the guiding light on what to do.

As an implementation specialist I am always aware of how knowing what to do and doing it are two different things. Just consider the high number of doctors who smoke, or how many people are trying to lose weight or get fit, with the emphasis on trying. I am always excited by peers who continuously develop new tools and techniques to continuously support leaders. The Personal Agility Lighthouse (PALH™) model with its seven agilities allows leaders to assess themselves and identify where they need to personally transform. This is critical because before you have organization agility you have to have personal agility.

The Personal Agility Lighthouse (PALH™) model guides leaders in their own personal transformation and prepares them to guide their organization at a time when every organization has to, to different extremes, transform to adopt digitalization. With so many new technologies all evolving at the same time, leaders are revisiting what their customer want and need. Why do we start with the customer? Because technology is not disrupting business, new customer requirements are. Technology is the means to deliver the new requirements. It's not about having a digital strategy but implementing a strategy in a digital world and Raji and Michal; the Personal Agility Lighthouse (PALH™) model guide leaders through the tricky and rocky path ahead where so many others are coming '**washed up**.'

Enjoy your own **Personal Agility** transformation journey!!

Foreword

Executive Director of Brightline Initiative
https://www.brightline.org/

How can you be successful in a world of permanent change and ever-growing challenges? In order to be truly successful and collaborate well with others, we need to develop a solid understanding of Personal Agility. Personal Agility it is not just about using the agile methodology. Being agile really starts with adopting a mindset that values urgency, having the emotional intelligence and leading in a way that recognizes that you are responsible for making your vision a reality.

The ***Personal Agility Lighthouse (PALH™) Model*** talks about seven sets of competencies and behaviors that each of us need to develop as effective leaders: Education Agility, Emotional Agility, Change Agility, Cerebral Agility, Political Agility, Learning Agility and Outcomes Agility. When I first came across the ***Personal Agility Lighthouse (PALH™) Model*** created by Raji Sivaraman and Michal Raczka, the founders of AgilityDiscoveries, I immediately drew a connection to Brightline's People Manifesto. The Brightline People Manifesto puts the focus back on the power of leadership in driving positive outcomes. It begins with you, the leader. It begins with your ability to be able to lead and step-back based on what the situation demands. It begins with your capability to craft the right mix of capabilities and skillsets, to architect a culture that is built on collaboration, transparency and accountability. A truly agile leader needs to continuously strive to create conditions and dialogs to make changes individually desirable and at the same time aligned with the broader interest. Organizational change starts with change at the individual level, and leaders do need to accept, live and embody this change.

If you are interested in being a successful leader, to become better at leading people, then developing Personal Agility should be on your agenda. This book is a great addition to the body of work on leadership and truly guides leaders on how to grow and develop others.

I am sure you will enjoy reading this book and apply it in practice just as the 10th principle of the Brightline Initiative says **"Celebrate success and recognize those who have done good work"**!!

"A project is complete when it starts working for you, rather than you working for it."

Scott Allen[1]

CHAPTER 1

Perspectives Through Personal Agility

In our minds, a project or an organization is all about the complexities in today's fast-paced, competitive, and dynamic environment. It does not matter what kind of projects or organizations we plunge into. It could be any industry: small, medium, large, or mega. Besides there being a lot of ambiguity, we need to deal with human behaviors. The biggest impact is on leadership skills that are talked about in the Project Management Institute article, *Navigating Complexity*.[2] From our perspective, *personal agility* with its seven flavors can positively influence the ability to manage complexities and this can be considered as an ultimate goal to deliver the expected projects' or organizations' outcomes.

In an ideal world, projects are linear and the project or the organization's performance is easy to measure. Keeping in mind our definition of the project/organization, the project or the organization's performance is in a predicament as projects are empirical and nonlinear endeavors. We cannot simply use measurements from the project management triple constraints (scope, cost, time).[3] We need to do a deep dive into more meaningful measurements, for example, stakeholders' and in particular customer's satisfaction, project team or an organization's happiness, just to name a few. In order to succeed as an organization or project team, we need to have a sense of purpose. This is not confined to projects only. In this context, we need to be aware of unfinished projects where we care about long-term products and value for customers, which encompasses the whole organization. The success for a team or an organization is to build great products and maintain sustainability. This can lead to a long-term sense of purpose and high performance measurements.

A high-performing project or an organization reaches the final outcome even though there might exist a myriad of complexities. It is all about achieving the highest level of outcomes agility. Complexity can be mastered through other agility flavors. Teams and organizations that want to master all or any of the agility flavors have much higher chances to deliver a high-performing organization, project, product, or deliverable. With its sense of purpose high-performing projects and organizations are all about delivering value, which entice customers and bring long-term satisfaction to the table.

Taking a look at the opposite horizon of the ocean, a low-performing project or an organization can be considered as one where a team or an organization is unable to deliver the ultimate goal, which is stakeholder satisfaction. This is notwithstanding the achievement of the basic Key Performance Indicators (KPIs) from the leaders' and managers' triple constraints theory mentioned above. This is where organizational agility needs to be ubiquitous for which the seven agilities will certainly chug the boats faster and efficiently.

~Education agility
  ~~Change agility
    ~~~Emotional agility
      ~~~~Political agility
        ~~~~~Cerebral agility
          ~~~~~~Learning agility
            ~~~~~~~Outcomes agility

Teams need to have the courage to measure a project or an organization's performance that are under a great level of involvedness. Teams need to constantly predict customer satisfaction or the Net Promoter Score,[4] and this is only possible through feedback loops. This courage of an individual to obtain feedback is a soft skill, which is perfectly addressed as an ability to hone *personal agility* flavors such as *Learning Agility*, *Change Agility*, and *Education Agility*. Project and organizational performance is undoubtedly all about *Outcomes Agility*.

One of the most important "game changers" in an agile organization is how you manage your performance system. Do you want to have a team or a group of people? It is very important how we manage goals and performance appraisals in a company.

What You Measure Is What You Get
WYMIWYG

The things that matter most at the workplace aren't measurable. You can't measure directly the level of trust among team members or the members of an organization at large, but that trust level powers everything that the teams and the entire organization does. We can't measure the degree to which team members want to be doing what they're doing but that element is essential to an organization's success. The same applies for *personal agility*. Although you cannot measure it directly, it plays a very important role when striving for performance. Personal agility is an understanding of agile mindsets in today's modern organizations. People say "be Agile, don't do Agile," but how can you know if you are already Agile? How can you measure it? You cannot improve what you cannot measure since a number value cannot be calculated nor an indicative formula can be put on the measurement of trust. The fourth point in a Forbes[5] article says: "If you can't measure something, you can't manage it." This is why our model is crucial in every sense—meaning 360 degrees.

A team or an organization is what you have when people have the same purpose and goals. This is obvious to understand but rare in many organizations. In most organizations, people and teams have individual goals. The manager gives an individual a set of goals and then, after some time, there is a performance appraisal. How, then, can cross-functional projects succeed when we have a group of people with individual goals from managers? Performance is a team sport, not an individual sport for organizations. Even if the leader or the project manager builds a team with a workshop defining organizational or project goals, this is not a system change and by the time performance appraisal is done, people will only think about their individual goals. This is because performance appraisal is conducted for a single person and not for the project.

To alleviate this problem constant checks with your team members about what their goals are need to be performed. This needs to be a regular checkpoint. To give a sample of why this is required, in the technology industry, there are ongoing discussions between business and IT. Technical people do not understand business people and vice versa. It is not that they use different language, but that each has different goals.

Another important aspect of goals that impact performance is how they are managed in a hierarchy. Strategy is realized through goals from the top. The challenge is to connect these different worlds: leaders of a team and members of other teams (e.g., the management team). We tend to put our team goals first. It is natural but also dangerous for companies. Strategy realization plans should be transparent. Individual goals and team goals should correspond to organizational strategy as written in a PMI article.[6] This correspondents to *Outcomes Agility.*

In our mind, honing the seven agilities of *education agility, change agility, emotional agility, political agility, cerebral agility, learning agility and outcomes agility* enlarges the probability of project and organizational success and elevated performance. Based on extensive experience and research the equilibrium in the seven *personal agility* flavors is the way to achieve high performance. There are seven different flavors of *personal agility.* It is important to keep all of them in balance. All the project team members need to know their current state of *personal agility* in an organization. Here we bring a huge, unique, and "one of a kind" value via the Personal Agility Lighthouse™ Index. This is a *self-analysis assessment* (see Appendix) where every project participant can learn more about himself/herself in an organization. To find out which agilities are already honed and which should be further developed, the project team members are provided with hints, tools, and methodologies on how to learn and get better at them. Thus the probability of achieving high performance increases for everyone in the organization.

There is no one or right way to implement the seven agilities. It all depends on the teams involved, the organizational structure, culture, maturity, and the projects' and the organizational goals. There are of course a few "exceptions to the rule" aspects of implementation teams that should be focused on. People with highly honed *personal agility* can create enhanced *Organizational Agility.* There are many people who are focused on organizations and at the same time forget about individuals. Personal Agility is all about focusing on those individuals who can and want to change organizations. Misunderstanding or trying to address *personal agility* via some other methodologies/procedures may or may not work. There are no shortcuts in terms of mastering the seven agilities.

One pitfall that should be considered and talked through is transparency of measurements and metrics while applying and expending the seven agilities. Another drawback is linked to the teams' and organization's awareness of customers' needs and wants. Teams need to distinguish what will pay off and what is just a whim. If individuals hold on to their beliefs, not wanting to grow with the organization in all the directions that the wind may take you, then there will be an eminent downfall.

If individuals discontinue and not use their learning ability, which happens to be a big part of the Personal Agility nuances, then it objectively resonates with what the World Economic Forum (WEF)[7] says about "Learnability." The WEF says: "It's time to take a fresh look at how we motivate, develop and retain employees. In this environment, learnability[8]—the desire and capability to develop in-demand skills to be employable for the long-term—is the hot ticket to success for employers and individuals alike." They further go on to explain in detail as shown in Figure 2 below.

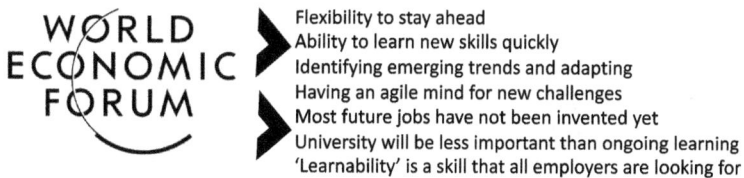

WORLD
ECONOMIC
FORUM

> Flexibility to stay ahead
Ability to learn new skills quickly
Identifying emerging trends and adapting
Having an agile mind for new challenges
Most future jobs have not been invented yet
University will be less important than ongoing learning
'Learnability' is a skill that all employers are looking for

Figure 2

Projects get off track every time project teams and organizations forget about clarity and continuous feedbacks. Without full self-expression and unambiguousness, teams tend to have their own sense of performance based on internal judgment of the project's and organization's KPIs (qualitative, quantitative, leading, and lagging). The organization and its teams can just disconnect from the project's stakeholders and thus can slip into low performance. Teams need to work in full limpidity mode by showing the product advancement and by measuring the KPIs together with stakeholders. The short cycle of product development, coupled with the constant availability of the services and products for customer evaluation and feedback, makes close interactions possible between the organization, teams, and the stakeholders. Although this will not prevent teams and the organization from pitching into a low-performance mode, it will unfold the progress very quickly. It can also unveil each and every stakeholders' involvement as they will want to give the feedback and their concerns sooner or later. Then by continuous adapting and adopting, the teams and the organization itself can have the possibility to get back on track. Adapting, adopting, and then adapting. This virtuous cycle is never ending for a high-performing organization as shown in Figure 3 below.

Raji Sivaraman and Michal Raczka 2019

Figure 3

"Sometimes you can't see yourself clearly until you see yourself through the eyes of others."

Ellen DeGeneres[1]

CHAPTER 2

---

antifragile

Education Agility

empathy

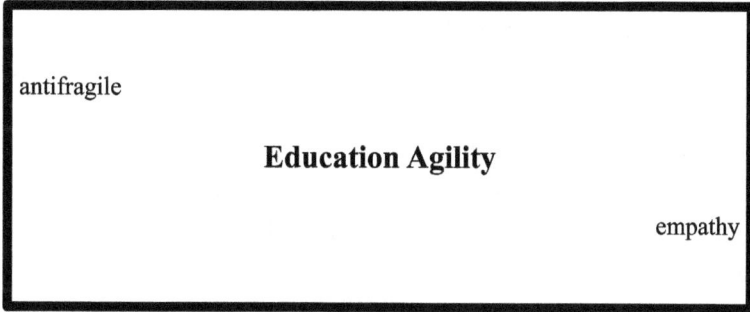

Education agility may also be called empathetic agility according to our opinion because it is distinctly different from emotions in many ways. Some examples are given below:

- Empathy is the ability to understand and share the feelings of another. Emotions are a natural instinctive state of mind deriving from one's circumstances, disposition, or relationships with others.
- Empathy occurs and leaves with no room for emotion, meaning when empathy takes place it happens at that moment, leaving no emotional room between the individual and the one who is empathized. It is not cognitive in nature. There is a sense of self-awareness that provides some necessary space between the two. The empathizer experiences the same suffering with the other. As a result, it allows the individual to be more helpful, understanding, and comprehending than the individual who cannot empathize another.
- Empathy is cultivated emotional reactions of an individual to the observed experiences of another.
- Empathy moves us to be more understanding and helps us to be better managers/leaders. Emotions do not.
- Empathy rides along with motivation. Emotions ride along with feelings.

Emotional agility is explained in depth in Chapter 5 of this book.

To be a success individually or organizationally, Jeff Sussna, founder and principal of Ingineering.IT says: "The DevOps Equation: Agility + Empathy = Quality."[2] This sums up pretty much the whole concept of antifragile.

Being antifragile warrants one to develop this agility and feel others' perspectives. Feeling the pain points of the person sitting in a different chair and doing the roles that do not necessarily fall into your daily routine make you loftier at performing all sorts of work and be better as a team player. This will put you in a worthy position when you need to be able to stand in for your peers. But your daily routine is your main competency.

We decided to include Education Agility in our model in order to highlight the need of improving our education. Education in this model in our minds is to highlight the need for new competencies, which can help us to perform different roles and easily adapt to changes. This then answers the question: "how ably can the individual communicate and work with others at all levels?"

We want to specifically distinguish **Education Agility** from **Learning Agility**. Education Agility helps us to master new competencies, helps us to see trends and changes around us. Learning Agility is how we validate hypothesis,[3] how fast we learn or fail. In order to learn and be more antifragile we need to be educated. We need to continuously master new competencies.

While keeping your competency at a constantly moving speed, the following gives an opportunity for diverse knowledge to develop into a superior focused experience:

- studying,
- communicating,
- learning,
- training.

This can lead to intelligent growth skills for the team and a challenging commitment in a passionate direction. These steer the course toward learning more about the varied needs and wants of multiple stakeholders to enhance the team performance of the project as well as the organization.

Here we need to mention the concept behind an antifragile person. The concept is called T-shaped skills or T-shaped persons,[4] as shown below in the diagram. "The concept of **T-shaped skills**, or **T-shaped persons** is a metaphor used in job recruitment to describe the abilities of persons in the workforce. The vertical bar on the letter **T** represents the depth of related skills and expertise in a single field, whereas the horizontal bar is the ability to collaborate across disciplines with experts in other areas and to apply knowledge in areas of expertise other than one's own."

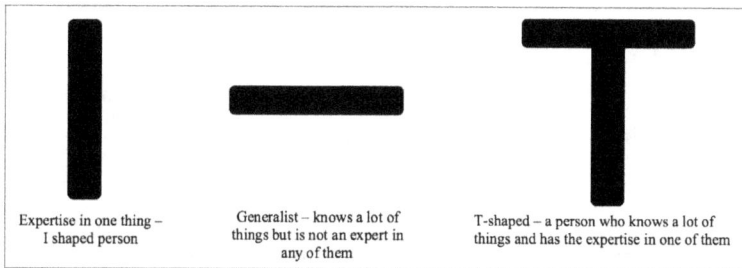

| Expertise in one thing – I shaped person | Generalist – knows a lot of things but is not an expert in any of them | T-shaped – a person who knows a lot of things and has the expertise in one of them |

Sourced from: https://medium.com/@jchyip/why-t-shaped-people-e8706198e437

Companies big and small, for example, Nike and Airbnb, are drawing on design thinking frameworks to jolt innovative ideas. In Design Thinking we use personas that are fictional characters, which you create based upon your research in order to represent the different user types that might use your service or product. Creating personas[5] helps us to understand our users' needs, experiences, behaviors, and goals. Creating personas can help us step out of ourselves and step into the other person's shoes. It can help us to recognize that different people have different needs and expectations, and it can also help us to identify with the user we're designing for.

Another example: Scrum Study[6] says that one of the core dimensions of collaborative work is: Awareness—Individuals working together need to be aware of each other's work. That weaves right into the Agile Manifesto value "**Customer Collaboration Over Contract Negotiation.**" In the sales arena, once the customers' needs, where they come from, as in gauging their mindsets, ethos, psyche, etc., and the customers' budgets are perceived and registered, a number of insights can then be steered into the lead generation dynamics. This is when customers can be turned into clients. Most often, the customers become one-time consumers, buyers, purchasers, etc., and do not evolve into clients. All of these can only be achieved and the performance of the projects and ultimately the organization reaches its zenith if this conversion passion is instilled throughout the entire team, which in turn will permeate to the entire organization. All the verticals must strive to be the best they can withering the darkest and wildest storms of the business nature, thus mandating *education agility*.

The idea that employees at Estee Lauder[7] have not only the training for one area but also the knowledge of a larger picture also allows them to succeed in areas that many may overlook. If an employee in Macy's is aware of how everything on a corporate level works they are more able to answer questions that in most instances would be sent to a customer service hotline. Allowing employees to have access to all sides of the company also helps with how they serve their customers. If they know the what, when, why, where, and how of the products and the company, they will be able to assist customers in all the situations much better.

To have the education agility honed, some of the remedies that can be employed are:

a) Be curious of other roles in their area of work. Seek out others with different perspectives.
b) Continuously strive and improve competencies through readings, trainings, mentoring, and coaching.
c) Find and follow people around you who inspire you, and use social media to follow them.
d) Expose yourself to new and challenging situations.
e) Know what you need and disrupt yourself. Give up what may have worked in the past.

Industry Applications by International Practitioners and Academia for Education Agility

Observation, empathy, understanding team values and synergy are crucial. Being able to put myself in the shoes of others helps me to cooperate more efficiently and to create a better, more satisfying relationship. I have learned that even if I seem to value direct feedback, not everyone can handle it, interpret it correctly and not take it personally. In our company, it is easy to see if you are empathetic to the client's needs or if you are treating the client as a necessary evil. Do you concentrate on being "right" or solving the problem, thus releasing the tension? These qualities are extremely important in employees dealing with clients directly. I have been educating and training my employees to fight for the client's interest rather than against it.

Joanna Staniszewska CEO, You'll Ltd.,
POLAND

Being flexible in dealing with others goes hand in hand with being flexible in developing educational skills that help you to excel in your work.

Makheni Zonneveld, Future Readiness Coach,
NETHERLANDS

Making sure that everybody understands, has the required intelligence and knowledge to then be able to recite and remember what portfolio management means for their business so that those who are educated can then do the educating.

Paul Hodgkins, Executive Director, Paul Hodgkins Project Consultancy,
UNITED KINGDOM

I always tell my students not be afraid to fail, be open to feedback, discover your strengths and build upon your weakness. Education should be a safe place where you can practice and improve your skills. Educating and being open to feedback builds character and competencies where you think you are lacking.

Professor Linh Luong, Program Director of Master of Science in Project
Management, University of SEATTLE

We are all aware that without education, without respect for others, we will never be able to work as a team. Education and respect within the organization and its diversity of cultures, is the basis and foundation of understanding and collaboration to join efforts in pursuit of the objectives set at the personal, group and organization level. Education Agility helps us to assess the needs of each of us, and also identify who within the group can supply that knowledge and help to the needed person to close the gap to further develop, execute and achieve the highest quality outcomes.

Rafael De La Rosa, Project-Portfolio Management Consultant,
PT. SMART tbk,
INDONESIA / SPAIN

New skills are required to take advantage of the data being generated. Increasingly, organizations are becoming less concerned with the volume of data and are (wisely) focusing on the context and relevance of data. Mastering education agility requires leaders to unlock those skills, analytical capabilities, and create multi-disciplinary and cross-functional skill-sets and insights to truly unlock the power of data.

Patrick N Connally, Director, Teradata, Philadelphia,
USA

Education Agility encompasses the adaptability to develop new competencies for future markets and the ability to foster T-shaped skills. It also helps in realizing the unrealized value as a result of exploring new possibilities of growth and outcomes. For improving the performance in the existing state-of-affairs, it requires continuous training and brilliance. When developing a cross-functional Scrum team having the capability to address different type of problems and identifying opportunities to build a business case, the agility demands the ability to solve the problems within the group working towards a common goal. It may require educating and motivating the peers to acquire new technical, professional or behavioral skills so that it builds a culture of constant evolution.

Gaurav Dhooper (PAL-I®, PMI-ACP®, SAFe4®, CSM®, LSS-GB)
Program Manager, RPA & Agile Practitioner at Genpact
INDIA

"Agility is fundamental to leading a team through times of change."

Sandra E. Peterson[1]

CHAPTER 3

last responsible moment

Change Agility

options

We feel that if one does not have the courage to take on challenges, actionable growth to hold the vision in sight may not be an option. This will result in a faulty combination of anxiety and excitement, which may bring down the performance of an organization. Flexibility in a communicative and adaptive approach to clients can be good to avoid collusion. Otherwise, one may not deal with changes pertaining to the customers, but only one's own changes. Decisive guidance creates excitement, hope, and energy to different changes that an open-minded environment recognizes for optimal team performance. This is why taking time for situations to evolve is much better than rushing to decisions.

We decided to have Change Agility in our model because it perfectly reflects what agile is about. It is about change, it is about feedback based on which we can create and respond aptly to that change.

While examining the fourth value from the Agile Manifesto, "**Responding to Change Over Following a Plan**," Ambysoft[2] writes: "Change is a reality of software development, a reality that your software process must reflect. There is nothing wrong with having a project plan. However, a project plan must be malleable, there must be room to change it as your situation changes otherwise your plan quickly becomes irrelevant." We opine that *change agility* works when we have options. One of the options is being able to change the plan as necessary.

Analyzing yourself to build a good foundation/base for oneself to help others, learning diverse cultures encourages adapting with others and within oneself and for others. This is a strong ability to adapt as a team. This reflection improves organizational changes in several ways. For example, when there are economic and political changes in the organizational environment internally and externally, rules and regulation changes are inevitable. This is where one can wait until the last responsible moment (LRM) to make decisions to cater for the changes. This means that this moment is when negative impact will occur and that moment is the last moment to take action and not delay any further.

Many companies use A/B testing[3] as an example of deferring commitment (LRM) and having options. "A/B testing is a method of comparing two or more versions of a product or process against each other to determine which one performs better. AB testing is essentially an experiment where two or more options of a product/service are shown to users at random, and statistical analysis is used to determine which option performs better for a given conversion goal." We leaders and teams should know how and when to use A/B testing to defer commitment, to test our options, and make decisions as late as possible. Another example of deciding as late as possible in agile development methods is the sprint planning, or iteration planning. In agile, we decide what features to include in each iteration and analyze them just in time for them to be developed. This enables us to have options and we can apply the "change agility" as leaders.

As a whole, the organizations' performance is going to change drastically. *Change agility* in our minds is the commanding force. For example, in Amazon,[4] the performance is going to depend on the employees and how they adapt to the new changes that is going to come about, because Amazon purchased Whole Foods. Many alterations are going to jerk the employees. There may be a few employees that are not going to want these amendments to occur because they are already used to the old rules and regulations that the company once had. Due to these changes that will surface, those employees who do not want variations will begin to react differently to the new owners and how they perform while doing their job.

In terms of scope and budget, the LRM concept borrowed from Lean thinking fits perfectly for the construction industry. Reaching the end goal as satisfaction of the customers and users can be achieved without much turbulence if one keeps in mind that commitment can be deferred to the point where nondecision moments will have a negative impact.

Having options is a luxury and in this particular case we need to have the cost of options in mind. During a construction project, it is vital to put intellectual efforts and decide if a building will have 10 or 20 floors. But there is little value in making decisions about the specifics of the 9th floor, for example. Here we need to use the architecture principles, which allow us to adapt to changing user requirements. For instance, developers should understand the KANO model (as shown below in Figure 4) of the customers' and users' satisfaction.

The Kano Model: Correlation of satisfaction drivers and investment needs

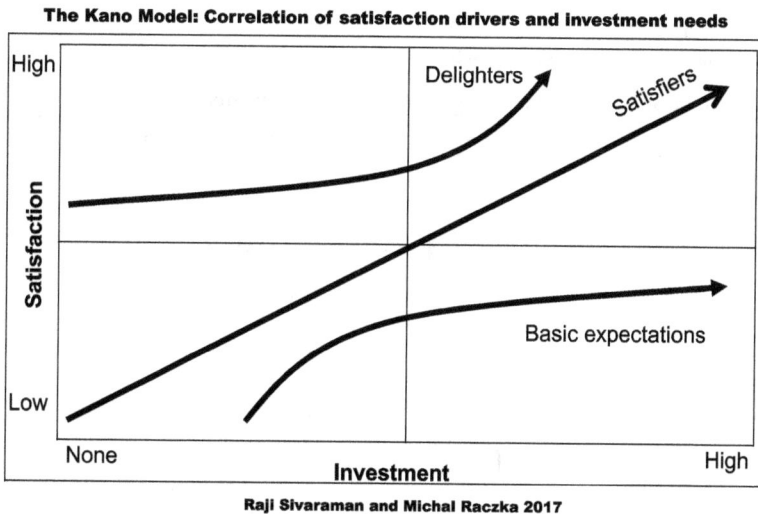

Raji Sivaraman and Michal Raczka 2017

Figure 4

This will give them the power and knowledge to make appropriate decisions and to figure out if decisions should be deferred or left open for further dialogue. Pushing for a fixed scope is not as advantageous as communicating clearly the next steps and points of decisions.

"The Kano Model[5] is an approach to prioritizing features on a product roadmap based on the degree to which they are likely to satisfy customers. Product teams can weigh a high-satisfaction feature against its costs to implement, to determine whether or not adding it to the roadmap is a strategically sound decision. Kano can help teams determine which features will satisfy and even delight customers. These feature categories can range from those that could disappoint customers, to those likely to satisfy or even delight customers. This strict focus on how customers will react to each feature distinguishes the Kano Model from other prioritization frameworks. With the Kano Model, the key consideration for any new feature is how much it will satisfy users."

To have the change agility honed, some of the remedies that can be employed are:

a) Respond quickly to the strategic opportunities presented by your environment, sector and market.
b) Listen to the voice of your customers and business partners.
c) Keep an eye on risks—changing quickly does not mean putting current company assets at risk.
d) Make sure to have contingency plans and options.
e) Anticipate and plan change—this needs to be part of your DNA.

Industry Applications by International Practitioners and Academia for Change Agility

Almost nothing changes as quickly as data. Data is fluid, changing with each new customer, transaction or social media account. While your data is changing, your stakeholders business needs are evolving. Strong data leaders are able to create and govern in a shifting environment.

Patrick N Connally, Director, Teradata, Philadelphia,
USA

I have learned that being in the present and paying attention to everything around me, helps me foresee and forecast the future. Connecting the dots aptly, actively listening to what people are saying and understanding their hesitation prepares me to anticipate and plan for obstacles and risks. These help me to figure out how to create options and manage expectations by only committing to what I truly understand because once the choices are clear, the decision is easy. It never ceases to amaze me how these small steps have helped the entire team become more efficient and productive. We have found ways to work collaboratively, find solutions and own responsibility. Being accountable and delighting our clients by delivering extremely complex projects on time is achieved due to honed change agility.

Joanna Staniszewska CEO, You'll Ltd.,
POLAND

We do not look at where we want to take our organisation to, what our vision is, where we want to get to and what possible options are available. As a consultant, one of the many management hypes is as long as the option promises cost-saving it is adopted without asking, 'If this is the answer, what was the question?' In the recycling project, the equipment does a great job of separating plastic from tin and glass but is that the desired outcome? That kind of thinking reflects change agility.

Makheni Zonneveld, Future Readiness Coach,
NETHERLANDS

Organisations which firstly agree and then recognise the need to adapt their portfolio, are demonstrating change agility. They choose wisely, they innovate when those moments of portfolio resource "stretch" come and they will always consider all of the portfolio options at their disposal when deciding what needs to be changed. In today's world where what happened an hour ago is already overtaken by what happened a minute ago, adaptability to the speed of change is the new constant by which business will either live or die. This is true for a businesses portfolio too.

Don't change and fall behind, don't change well and fall behind further and just like with agile, you really don't want to fall behind in a series of sprints.

Paul Hodgkins, Executive Director, Paul Hodgkins Project Consultancy,
UNITED KINGDOM

As part of any problem solving, we also have to think about how to adjust our actions in order to meet our goals. Education reflects the needs of the business world, thus evolving with the needs of the customers. Educators have to be thoughtful in what to design/educate in order to develop the personal skills of future professionals and leaders.

Professor Linh Luong, Program Director of Master of Science in Project
Management, University of SEATTLE

An organization focusing more on predictability will try to minimize and control the changes and will always look for alternatives to avoid the impact on current product capabilities so that cost and effort can be saved as the contract is fixed in nature. Whereas, an adaptable organization will allow such changes to happen in terms of supporting future needs of the business and market through agile contracts to stay competitive, evolve the product capabilities and deliver customer value at a sustainable pace even during the period of uncertainty and ambiguity.

Gaurav Dhooper (PAL-I®, PMI-ACP®, SAFe4®, CSM®, LSS-GB)
Program Manager, RPA & Agile Practitioner at Genpact
INDIA

Change agility must be carried out at all times; since it is necessary during the life cycle of our products, from the Business Case to operation. Its homonym in traditional Project management would be the process of "Perform Integrated Change Control". Our organization must be agile in making decisions when options are provided. Currently we are not making decisions when they are required. This situation creates a negative impact to the expected benefits of our projects, therefore deriving poor main stakeholders' satisfaction. Our Department structure wants to set up to optimize consensus or the decision-making process. This is where I think Change Agility can help us find the right organizational structure where people have real end-to-end ownership, a holistic leadership.

Rafael De La Rosa, Project-Portfolio Management Consultant,
PT. SMART tbk
INDONESIA / SPAIN

"You can focus on things that are barriers or you can focus on scaling the wall or redefining the problem."

Tim Cook[1]

CHAPTER 4

cognitive improvisations

Emotional Agility

responsiveness

Emotional Agility is to develop an understanding of the relationship between moods, thoughts, behaviors and then to take charge of them by practicing skills to cope with intense negative feelings, extreme sadness, anxiety, anger, and so on and so forth. One broadens oneself via awareness, coping skills, regulating difficult feelings, killing skepticism, and tolerating challenging situations in setting goals. When one has the capability to take control of these behavioral changes in oneself, the teams get solidified, the department becomes steady, and ultimately the organization's success will peak. That is the reason we decided to add Emotional agility into our model.

Emotional intelligence and partnership in government visibility and innovation can be smooth sailing if this particular flavor is honed in. An example to illustrate is the invasion of Cuba by President Kennedy and his advisors. As we know it failed. One of the reasons is because when there is a groupthink in process, there are disagreements that are bound to happen. Sometimes in these scenarios, the majority opinions are taken as the actions to go ahead with and issues raised by minority individuals are not dealt with. This happens in small, medium, and large organizations too. So individuals as well as companies have to make sure the emotional behavior of the individuals and the group is geared toward the organizational goal.

Emotional Agility warrants agile appearances and sometimes suppression of inner feelings. Psychological adaptability and cognitive improvisations under stress create anticipating changing situations. This includes obstacles, tidal waves that an organization may encounter due to multiple organizational acquisitions. An individual may arise to a nonprogrammed decision. In this scenario, emotional agility would, without a doubt, be a great trait to have, to utilize in unusual, unpredictable opportunities and threats such as these.

Dealing with disgruntled customers, different temperaments, lies, anxiety, the customers' needs, manipulation, lack of patience, and much more in an organizational setting can be handled very delicately with our definition of *emotional agility*. To cite a few immediate remedies for an organization's performance brilliance, we suggest instilling enthusiasm for the work with motivational organizational rides such as friendliness in and around the work space that boosts their morale. Inculcating compassion toward the team and beyond added with indoctrinating balancing work and life hours will certainly have emotions at a calm level.

Jiten Vara in Scrum and Kanban[2] says: "There are absolute advantages to having tools and processes, but if we really want to create awesome software and come to work where both us and our clients are happy then we should probably focus on the people and spend a bit more time understanding how people interact and communicate." Taking the Agile Manifesto value **"Individuals and Interactions over Processes and Tools"** concept this is where *emotional agility* intertwines in tandem.

Having the patience to bear the pains of an organization involves ardent listening, fellow feeling to cope with fear. Self-awareness in many arenas is a staple for *emotional agility*. For example, summing up productive indications for short- and long-term planning, making sure that the customers' curiosity requirements, not just the BRD (Business Requirement Documents), are addressed in a timely and satisfactory manner. This helps to overcome the rough and extreme state of affairs with multiple organizational acquisition dealings. On the flip side, customer curiosity within reason if not curbed can make the project performance sway unnecessarily.

Just to give a simple example, some of the mainstays of tenacity of the sales and imports team according to us are as stated here. Implanting the push for incite and drive throughout the entire team to be the best they can by talking through a tiresome conflict resolution setting, and not getting personal. Team excellence and success for career with a passion for complete transparency of the weekly Profit & Loss results and how this impacts the organizational goals and the annual profit pledge is at its high tide here.

To take another case, Urban Outfitters[3] does not just end their training after the day is done. Instead, there is an application (app) for Urban Outfitters employees to see how they are progressing in the company. The app also helps decide whether employees and teams are promoted or are going to stay at the level they are at. The app shows transparency and transparency helps build trust among workers within a company or external to the organization. The app shows the logistics and rational mindset of the company. With transparency, there is very little room to withhold information and to lie to their personnel. This is one of the main reasons individuals choose to work at Urban Outfitters.

The designing and processes of the app include making sure that the app runs efficiently and effectively.
This also includes:

- making sure that every bit of information is updated,
- is easy to use,
- making sure that employees are using the app to ensure that all the designing and development is worth the time in building and updating the app.

The app helps in the reflection of the individual as well as the team because it shows how many sales they have made and their progress during a certain time period. If Urban Outfitters employees maintain a certain number of sales then it is a good reflection of the company. By including this app, Urban Outfitters, as a company, has kept a transparent relationship between their corporation and their employees, due to past mistakes that were made.

To have the emotional agility honed, some of the remedies that can be employed are:

a) Being friendly in and around the work space even though there might be drifts.
b) Making sure the requirements that the stakeholders have are not out of curiosity but out of genuine need for the product or the contract negotiated.
c) Responsiveness and understanding go beyond one's own team, extending to other verticals and departments of the organization.
d) For collaborations emotions cannot come in the way of navigating to the intended results.

Industry Applications by International Practitioners and Academia for Emotional Agility

Some of the most agile organisations use emotional agility; they improvise, they know how they feel about the decisions they need to make as to the portfolio's governance and they consistently apply appropriate and professional behaviours when doing so.

Paul Hodgkins, Executive Director, Paul Hodgkins Project Consultancy,
UNITED KINGDOM

Having the openness to learn and change increase our emotional agility. Awareness of our emotional intelligence in relationship to others provides an adaptability to change, reasoning, coping, and increases our ability to problem solve while understanding the complexity of a non-linear problem. Today's complexity of real world business problems affects our political, personal, and social environment taking in gray areas of consideration. Emotional agility is required in order to recommend a solution at the table.

Professor Linh Luong, Program Director of Master of Science in Project
Management, University of SEATTLE

At the senior management level, when things go wrong, usually and most often exploiting, hurting feelings of people who are giving their best and are not really guilty of the situation and not responsible of the negative deviations of the plan becomes a norm. This can be avoided with the application of Emotional agility.

Rafael De La Rosa, Project-Portfolio Management Consultant,
PT. SMART tbk
INDONESIA / SPAIN

While there is a strong mental connection to data, the emotional connection to data cannot be underestimated. Data tells stories, and sometimes, ugly stories about the (sad) reality of their current or future state. Data is also highly personal. Within organizations, fiefdoms and data kingdoms can arise – HR doesn't want to share certain data elements; marketing may need and want to understand or leverage key operational / sales data, and the IT group may feel an overall ownership / stewardship over all enterprise data. These challenges and organizational silos require leaders to have high emotional IQs, specifically the ability to adapt, improves and manage numerous stakeholder groups.

Patrick N Connally, Director, Teradata, Philadelphia,

USA

During the period of organizational transformation, it is pertinent that people adapt to change organically and thrive which happens only when the purpose and goal are clearly explained by the leaders. Leaders also need to coach people if required and gain the buy-in from the target audience. One of the important values of Scrum process framework is "Respect" which allows Scrum team to build a professional culture and makes the team emotionally intelligent.

Emotional agility is to be sharpened in order to achieve futuristic success. Here, we have to consider both current value and unrealised/ future value. The goal of looking at the current value is to maximize the value that an organization delivers to customers and stakeholders at any given time; it considers not only what exists right now, but the value that might exist in the future as well as continuous improvement and continuity is the name of the game in the agile world.

Gaurav Dhooper (PAL-I°, PMI-ACP°, SAFe4°, CSM°, LSS-GB)

Program Manager, RPA & Agile Practitioner at Genpact

INDIA

Juggling your associates and their different emotional states can be difficult. Being able to convince a skeptic, comfort and uplift a sad person, motivate, encourage others to stop being shy simultaneously can be quite a rollercoaster. But, the good news is that you can be trained.

The first step is to evaluate yourself. How stable and calm you are in a stressful situation. What is your ability to read a situation and diffuse it if needed and how self-controlled are you when faced with adversity? The best I gather from the PALH^{TM} model for this agility is to say, "Take your drama somewhere else! I don't want to put my team through the unwanted stress of having to go through unnecessary emotional tensions." The team needs to know that their leader has everything under control. Helping the team to manage their emotions is possible when you are able to manage your own. Although, at times I did allow them to witness my inner hesitation because that made them understand that regardless of how tough it got, I almost always put the team first and that would allow them to see that I am human too.

Joanna Staniszewska CEO, You'll Ltd.,
POLAND

We cannot wish away the fact that the whole person, emotions and all, comes to work. Emotional agility helps us to be flexible in dealing with our own emotions and with the emotions of others. Situations like challenging the person who introduces a recycling equipment that separates paper from glass when that is not the desired outcome will lead to friction and that is where emotional agility stands you in good stead.

Makheni Zonneveld, Future Readiness Coach,
NETHERLANDS

"When something is important enough, you do it even if the odds are not in your favour."

Elon Musk [1]

CHAPTER 5

---

collaborative contribution

Political Agility

sustainability

For business value to grow, Political Agility is a necessary sail. It emerges with distinctive divide, may it be between individuals, varied stakeholders, departments, countries, other entities, etc. Perfect alignment is never a possibility, so avoiding overbearing, overriding conflicts with rationalistic and ideological waves will guide an individual and an organization to make the right choices with persistence, dedication, and collaborative contribution. As such, it was logical to have Political Agility in our model as it is roiled by emotions and to nullify the negative effects it brings with the churning, we feel Political Agility certainly needs to be honed.

Politics is everywhere and it is a known fact that Machiavellianism is not going to vanish anytime soon. Upper management calls the shots sometimes without assessing the outcomes and its risks. One such example is when the space shuttle Challenger was launched. Morton Thiokol Incorporated and NASA wanted to prove to the public the success of the US space program so that they could get future funding. They did not ensure the safety of the astronauts, thus ending up losing all seven crew members. Therefore, every individual and every organization needs to hone political agility just as we see in this example where expert technical advice was not taken into consideration and in fact speaking up was discouraged. An individual of expertise needs to be given the thumbs-up to share the findings and organizational decisions weighed ethically with inputs gathered from all parties. In short, politics and its demerits can be very harmful to organizations. This is why political agility is very important for an organization's projects, portfolios, programs, and much more to come to apt consensus before embarking on endeavors, especially of this rare nature.

"Performance with a Purpose" has been talked about in so many international forums by many C levels. It brings power, order, loyalty, ethics, trust, emotion, culture, and communication to the desired shores of that organization. When people in an office are calm, cohesive, and are full of integrity, corporate caution that is so inevitable can be managed in an easier way. If profit is the only objective, obstacles such as gossip, being cut-throat, etc., will demean the leadership quality desired in an organization. Instead, tactfulness and leading by example can negate the loss, and the ability to deliver minimum satisfactory result for pointless activities is what we feel is the essence of *political agility*.

Mishkin Berteig in agileadvice[2] writes this thought about this Agile Manifesto value: "**Individuals and Interactions over Processes and Tools**" is basically a statement that given the right circumstances we can use processes and tools, but that our default approach to work and problem-solving should be to focus on individuals and their interactions. Processes and tools do not improve on their own.

As such in our minds the brightest beams that will guide toward *political agility* are when utmost caution is exercised with the corporation. This ship can be landed safely ashore with the quality of the leaders that navigate with far-sighted and near-sighted vision in mind. Saying and doing exactly as the leaders would want their teams and projects to perform is one way of attaining this. In other words, *leading by example*. One such example is to weigh all options and then support the decision-making right down from the bottom of the sea. A robust action chain is vital for any organization's performance to reach the desired shores. This should encompass a minimum of:

- expecting probable glitches,
- intervening before corrective action is indispensable,
- attitudes and actions of leaders' deeds and conducts to be cognizant.

When all of these are ploughed through a chain reaction, there will be no link that has a chance to break in the chain. These measures above will be the guiding force for responsive sustainability of the empowerment of all the stakeholders in a project and all situational topographies.

One of the key parameters of the agile supply chain management[3] is to make sure that there is as less friction as possible within and around the supply chain cosmos. In the article, Muhammad Sher says, "To make it robust chain, it would be vital to use state of the art, planning applications, that supports the working teams in decision making and sometimes with what if scenario capability, usually companies go for backup plans that costs considered to be extra, than such applications make it more responsive and cost efficient."

Political Agility in our minds is the ability to navigate through competing agendas and collecting consensus among all stakeholders. This is a reality that all supply chain managers go through in their daily work routines. The credibility of these managers' viewpoints needs to be supported by the collection of evidence and the analysis of data to avoid political collision. Data pertaining to their own chains are available from their Enterprise Resource Planning (ERP) systems, logistics track & trace systems, and other integrated Business Warehouse Systems. External data are made available from portals such as Clearmetal and by using portals such as Flexport, Haven, or Infor for freight movement.

The industry of analyzing an organization may require establishing solid relationships from the get-go. Creative solutions to political dilemmas and getting the buy-in may require individuals to be involved with an agile mindset. This may be attained when individuals work independent of politics at every single strata, situation, project, team, and so on and so forth. So the queries here for the personal agility of an individual to reach up to organizational agility will be "How come," "How much," and "How not to" as shown in Figure 5 on next page.

Political Agility for Organizational Agility

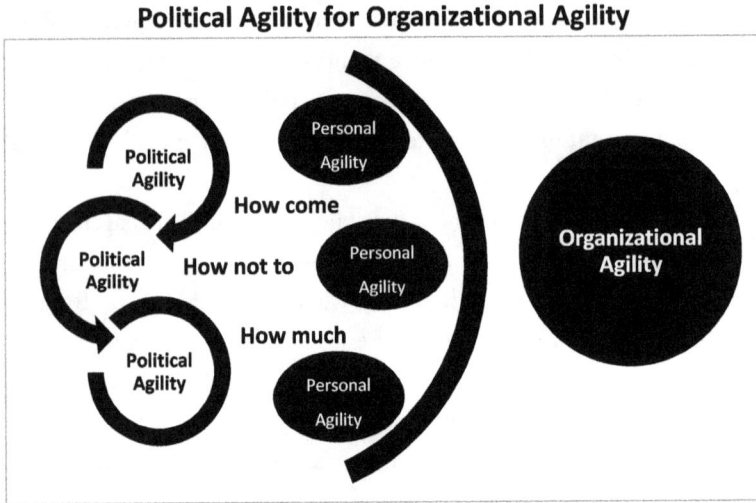

Raji Sivaraman and Michal Raczka 2017

Figure 5

Figure 5 above highlights the essential questions to ask oneself: How come the situation came to this point? How much damage is already done and how much can be avoided so that one can find out how not to damage even more and how not to have a repeat performance. Extrapolating some of the points from "Rebecca Knight,"[4] these queries when answered by each individual to full satisfaction pave the path from personal agility to organizational agility.

Honing political agility can be done in a number of ways. A few ways are given below:

Upper management can:

a) Lead by example.
b) Support innovative decisions made by all levels in the organization.
c) Set sail into the corporate seas with cautionary efforts.
d) Respond to the political challenges need to be effective and sustainable for the growth and development of an organization.

Industry Applications by International Practitioners and Academia for Political Agility

As long as there is more than one person in any situation, politics are inevitable. Political agility helps you to survive organizational politics. When external stakeholders like service providers are involved, the relationships between internal stakeholders may be affected because the person who introduces the external stakeholder may either have personal interest or take the objection to the idea as a personal attack. Political awareness and cautiousness helps you to win the other person not to your side but to the side of the interest of your organization.

Makheni Zonneveld, Future Readiness Coach,
NETHERLANDS

The best way to gain your team's and your partner's trust is to be ethical at all times. It takes years to build a relationship, to build confidence, to construct a reputation. But, it takes less than a moment to lose it all. I recently had this situation where I stopped trusting a close business partner, who I thought was family. I am sure, the whole team will never forget the day I confronted them. But if my teams trust me, they will stand behind my decision and support me. Political agility certainly paved the way in this instance.

Joanna Staniszewska, CEO, You'll Ltd.,
POLAND

The aim of political agility is to create an environment of trust and transparency for achieving the organization growth. It also requires changing the existing ways of working, if required to adopt pragmatic approaches to make the process leaner instead of continuing with bureaucratic style of functioning. The benefit of political agility is increased accountability amongst the team working towards a shared goal. An example could be the leadership communication during client interactions for supporting their team's decisions and approaches for achieving the customer outcomes. To aid to hone political agility, it may be worthwhile to look into the Cynefin framework (https://en.wikipedia.org/wiki/Cynefin_framework) shown in the diagram below. It is useful in responding to complex and chaotic problems through sensing the context and helps in avoiding the problems that arise when the preferred style causes to make mistakes. This is a key tool for creating agile leadership and resilient organizations.

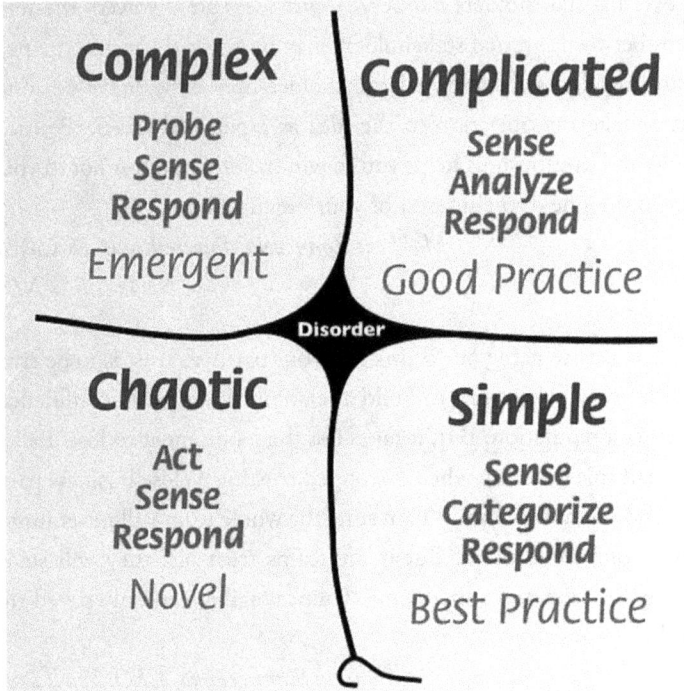

Complex

Probe
Sense
Respond

Emergent

Complicated

Sense
Analyze
Respond

Good Practice

Disorder

Chaotic

Act
Sense
Respond

Novel

Simple

Sense
Categorize
Respond

Best Practice

Source: https://commons.wikimedia.org/wiki/File:Cynefin_framework,_February_2011_(2).jpeg.

Gaurav Dhooper (PAL-I®, PMI-ACP®, SAFe4®, CSM®, LSS-GB)
Program Manager, RPA & Agile Practitioner at Genpact
INDIA

It could be argued they are demonstrating political agility; being ruthless as to what is no longer expedient and being gentle with what now is......how many times have you seen a politician change their opinion when the 'winds blow with or against them'?

Paul Hodgkins, Executive Director, Paul Hodgkins Project Consultancy,
UNITED KINGDOM

Our education system is steep in tradition and process. In order to understand the nuances and practice, one needs to understand the stakeholders involved, their objectives, the organizational strategies and goals, as well as where the customer's needs are. Like many organizations, challenges exist in how departments are structured and leadership power vacillates. Maneuvering through organizational structure, process and resources takes political agility.

Professor Linh Luong, Program Director of Master of Science in Project Management, University of SEATTLE

While the data may be simple, generating, and sustaining, political consensus on the value of data may be any data analysts' biggest challenge.

Patrick N Connally, Director, Teradata, Philadelphia, USA

My personal opinion is that politics is the only universal religion, where, in all countries and cultures, it is established and rooted since prehistoric times. There are different types of politics and politicians, but both are moved by two rules: ***governability*** (countries, organizations, people, etc.), and ***decisions***, which are taken based on political reasons and interests. In our company many decisions depend on internal politics and interests of groups with greater strength within the organization, even though I must say that company owners are doing and giving a great support to catch up with the "disruptive technologies" that nowadays are changing our life and business models. In particular, in our department, Political Agility can help us to become more aware and be more cautious in having an agile governability. Meaning, by taking the right decisions would benefit all stakeholders involved in our daily work activities, so that conflicts that may occur, for various reasons, are handled with persistence, dedication, collaborative and consensual contribution.

Rafael De La Rosa, Project-Portfolio Management Consultant, PT. SMART tbk, INDONESIA / SPAIN

"If you want to reach your goals and dreams, you cannot do it without discipline."

Lee Kuan Yew[1]

CHAPTER 6

> linear thinking
>
> ## Cerebral Agility
>
> complexity

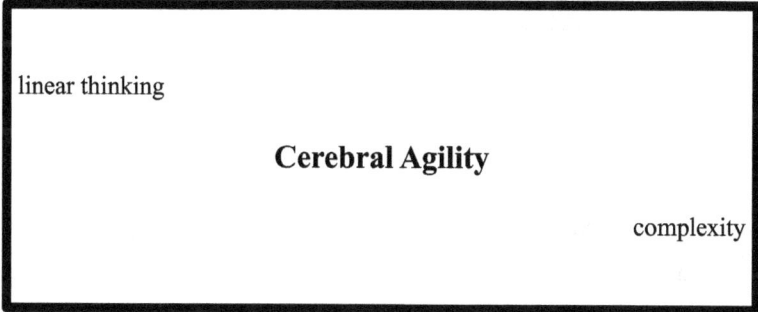

To reduce mental fatigue, reduce anxiety, and support healthy brain function of any individual, a clear intellectual thought is imperative. Efficiency and alertness combined with a sharp risk response mitigation is supported by this sailboat cerebral agility.

A very interesting concept that was written by Bart de Langhe, Stefano Puntoni, and Richard Larrick in the *Harvard Business Review* article "Linear Thinking in a Nonlinear World"[2] comes to mind here. Their powerful sentence is given below:

"This is true for generalists and specialists alike, because even experts who are aware of nonlinearity in their fields can fail to take it into account and default instead to relying on their gut."

This concept anchors deep into the T-shaped analogy given in Chapter 2 (Education Agility). While it is good to be an expert and a generalist, when there is a crisis, an environment that was not forecasted or foreseen on the horizon, anticipated codes or responses envisioned may not be deployable. Relying on one's cerebrum and its multitude of capabilities saves the day, the organization, and ultimately every stakeholder. It is synonymous to the waterfall vs agile mindsets in a way. This is why we decided to include Cerebral Agility in our model.

There are times when you are stuck because there is a situation where you are at a loss as to how to answer or act or come up with solutions. In this moment, you have to give yourself time to think but you don't have much time and what comes out of your mouth has to be Persuasive, Powerful, Credible, and Informative.

An organization thrives when there is a steady stream of think tanks looking for new ways to make the organization more efficient, responsive, and creative, to say the least. Obscure situations need quick responses—Emergency Room doctors need to think fast—cerebral agility is at its height here. Lives are at stake here. It is the same when there is a sudden explosion, hostage situations, fire, etc.

This kind of environment needs to be created in an organization to facilitate this agility. Highly innovative companies like Facebook, Ikea, Apple, and many more give their employees and temporary teams the freedom to make these decisions and develop and create new and innovative ideas. All organizations no matter whether they are a startup or been around for ages, in such scenarios, need to cultivate this environment as well.

Cerebral Agility fetches new viewpoints, shows ease in difficult and obscure situations, coming up with timely guidance. Here is the mantra that combines the ingredients to maturity—know more, read more, be curious—therein lies your adaptive achievement! When you want to have good ideas you need to have many ideas. Having options and ideas is a luxury. Keeping it in a repository radar screen, monitoring, generating more ideas to use, and gauging the ideas as and when it is needed. When we manage projects, we need to build interdisciplinary project teams that are able to generate new ideas and options on how to deliver consensus-driven projects.

Taking insights from "Julian Birkinshaw"[3] we can further define and explore this agility as the "action-oriented organizations." If one takes an organizational chart of any company, the structure shows various departments at the functional, departmental, and C-levels being responsible for different areas of the company. In the same manner, the cerebrum has different duties taken care of by varied sections. If there is perfect 360-degree integration, meaning all of the moving parts are coordinated and the boat is rowed in perfect rhythm by all the individuals, the success level of an organization is bound to be high. If one of the sections is amiss, therein comes the cerebral agility to make things right, as is the case for any organization where an outside consultant is called in or an in-house remedy is sought and implemented.

The capability of being agile in the moment makes the personal agility attributes expand itself to organizational agility. As is with individuals who are trendsetters, increasing the globalization of business with their out-of-the-box thinking. The dynamic complexity of how the brain and the mind work is quite simply genius, to put it mildly. So to cruise all the way from personal agility to organizational agility, the thoughts need to be at premortem, postmortem and the actual exercise of adoption, adaption levels within an individual and the organization in itself. It would be highly prudent to be revisiting these thought processes when taking the strides for each implementation. This will then lead to the adaption, adoption, adaption cycle to be sharpened.

Learning as you go with curiosity and being productive as an edifying endeavor with ideas formed out of brainstorming leads to imaginative creativity. Being brave during an urgency situation and having the boldness to be adaptive and clear at a circumstance thrown at a moment's notice is what *cerebral agility* is all about. Performance for "on-the-spot projects" evidently needs this agility to be a triumph. To emerge as a success solution provider, cerebral agility thus needs a project's and the organization's stakeholders to have creativity and imagination at its helm. Whether it is a project, program, or portfolio management, when emergency conditions and states arise, team thinking skills, efforts to hasten clarity in such extreme circumstances, and inventive work are mandatory. Both dexterity and proficiency are to be honed as well. Some examples for achieving these are by:

- brain exercises,
- role-plays,
- drills,
- scenario modeling.

No one can be fully prepared for these extenuating situations. Here bravery and logic should prevail amidst the boldness to be adaptive to save the day miraculously.

Just as in the Information technology world the Agile Manifesto says **"Working Software Over Comprehensive Documentation,"** cerebral agility is of utmost importance when it comes to saving the unknown. All the documentations, processes, tools, methodologies, and so on and so forth in the world cannot bring back the life of a project. This is on the grounds that the minds and brains of the teams and individuals are not working in sync and thinking out of the box with the unusual and out of the norm situation at hand. Moreover, as the explanation of this agile manifesto goes, programmers would rather code than document. People and teams that are truly dedicated to the success of the projects and the organization's performance want to find extraordinary ways to put the emergency situation back on the right track. They would rather try not to use the documented methods and sources. That will be a waste of time, energy, resources, etc.

"Over the years we have learned that if we asked people to rely on logic and common sense instead of on formal policies, most of the time we would get better results, and at lower cost. If you are careful to hire people who will put the company's interests first, who understand and support the desire for a high-performance workplace, 97% of your employees will do the right thing. Most companies spend endless time and money writing and enforcing HR policies to deal with problems the other 3% might cause. Instead, we tried really hard to not hire those people, and we let them go if it turned out we'd made a hiring mistake. Adult like behavior means talking openly about issues with your boss, your colleagues, and your subordinates. It means recognizing that even in companies with reams of HR policies, those policies are frequently skirted as managers and their reports work out what makes sense on a case-by-case basis" says the company Netflix.[4] This clearly draws full light into our *cerebral agility* beam because Netflix has statistics that show the reason why they are so insistent on high performance. They say, "In procedural work, the best are 2x better than average. In creative/inventive work, the best are 10x better than the average, so there is huge premium on creating effective teams of the best."

To have the cerebral agility honed, some of the remedies that can be employed are:

a) Take a deep breath and think before you act or speak.
b) Exercise the entire cerebrum with brain games regularly to be agile at all times.
c) Gear for nonlinear conditions even if linear circumstances are the norm in one's space.
d) Don't let deviations that cannot be avoided no matter how uncomfortable to outsmart us just as the paleomammalian cortex is inseparable from the prefrontal cortex.

Industry Applications by International Practitioners and Academia for Cerebral Agility

One outcome that we want students to achieve is "critical thinking." Learning to think critically is such an important skill. We use it every day to problem solve, critically analyze data, and how we can create meaningful communication in our organization to get our message across. This is the type of skill that business emphasize for hiring high performance employees.

Professor Linh Luong, Program Director of Master of Science in Project Management, University of SEATTLE

Having constant focus on organizational goals keep the creativity alive and allows the brain to think in a non-linear way by identifying, understanding and commiserating with the customer to come up with quick, clear, precise and to the point solution especially in a 'out of the box' situation. Design Thinking approach requires cerebral agility to build human-centric solutions. Cerebral agility helps in achieving higher degree of innovation through idea generation and critical thinking. It ties in with the "Time-to-market" - Expresses the organization's ability to quickly deliver new capabilities, services, or products. The goal of looking at 'Time-to-Market' is to minimize the amount of time it takes for the organization to deliver value.

Gaurav Dhooper (PAL-I®, PMI-ACP®, SAFe4®, CSM®, LSS-GB)
Program Manager, RPA & Agile Practitioner at Genpact
INDIA

This agility helps us to develop the best we have inside ourselves. In our sector, we can embrace Cerebral Agility as a process that helps us to be more curious, develop the best in us, generate and provide new ideas and alternatives in our organization. These processes when adapted quickly and agilely to the changes and trends of our market can bring the organizational agility to its peak.

Rafael De La Rosa, Project-Portfolio Management Consultant,
PT. SMART tbk
INDONESIA / SPAIN

Data (analytics) is highly cerebral. Data is factual, and binary. It tells a concrete story. Putting data to good use requires a critical analysis of current data needs, and data gaps. Absent this insight, organizations will struggle to build and communicate meaningful stories about the impact of their data analysis.

Patrick N Connally, Director, Teradata, Philadelphia,
USA

Being cerebrally agile means being able to gauge the circumstance, modify behaviour and deliver the right information at the spur of the moment. For me, part of this comes naturally and partly I have trained myself. As the head of an agency it is important for me to make quick situational decisions about whether it is possible to accomplish the project at a given time, will it be profitable, what competencies will I need to complete it successfully, and where to find the right people at the affordable cost?

An example in my company would be to be Agile 360 (**Agile360** degree **feedback** allows each individual to understand how agile an employee, coworker or staff member is viewed by others.). There was an instance where we needed subcontractors asap. What I did was to have the whole company brainstorm and bring to the table all the contractors we had used in the past and whoever had any connections with contractors. This emerged to be a great solution as we did solve the problem. It is just spontaneous thinking with the right resources.

Joanna Staniszewska CEO, You'll Ltd.,
POLAND

You achieve results when your brain and your mind work in an agile manner. This takes effort. We need to constantly train our minds by being curious, finding out more, reading more and learning to generate new ideas. That is where cerebral agility comes in.

Makheni Zonneveld, Future Readiness Coach,
NETHERLANDS

It's all about the right strategic projects, being undertaken at the right moment in time and for the right reasons whilst also accepting that those self same right projects, still have the capacity (through no fault of their own necessarily), to deliver the wrong results.

Paul Hodgkins, Executive Director, Paul Hodgkins Project Consultancy,
UNITED KINGDOM

"Learning to fly is not pretty but flying is."

Satya Nadella[1]

CHAPTER 7

microservice

Learning Agility

discovery

Quoting Renee Troughton from AGILE FOREST[2]: "Think about how the team may feel knowing that there is four months of work hanging over their heads. They are unlikely to feel inclined to innovate knowing that there is so much that the product owner still wants delivered." This is when the mindset has to change to "I don't know how, let me learn." Admitting ignorance is what this agility brings light to the Agile Manifesto, **"Working Software Over Comprehensive Documentation."**

Fulfillment and exploration need courage plus new intelligence. Discovering values and needs from the beginning by active participation and understanding the basics takes you to the top. To grow, openness and ideas afresh are paramount. Once an individual admits ignorance generating interest within oneself and actively participating to keep up with the trends for new discoveries, that then brings fresh and valid values for an organization. The ache to learn more constantly and the willingness not to ebb is a trait that every organization has to condition their teams and employees with. Leaders and managers with strong *learning agility*, always willing to learn new information can rapidly study, analyze, and understand new situations. New business problems to understand difficult challenges can strengthen innovative possibilities by making fresh connections.

Agility is about trying new things and discovering new areas, which can help people to become better. We decided to include Learning Agility in our model because it is fundamental to be open to new learnings and experiments. This is when we can start formulating our hypothesis and make them real, valuable, and impactful. Learn and check high-potential hypothesis fast. As an example of how to make Learning Agility easy, we can introduce Design Sprint which was developed by Google Ventures. The design sprint[3] is a five-day process for answering critical business questions through design, benchmarking, prototyping, and testing ideas with customers. Design Sprint is a shortcut to learn without building and launching. Many huge brands like Slack, PwC, etc., use Design Sprint.

> **When we learn fast, and check our hypothesis fast, we can also fail fast and failure is just the beginning. Failure creates new opportunities to learn.**

A fairly new concept Amazon has pursued is physical grocery stores, such as their own store in Seattle and their purchase of Whole Foods. "Whole Foods has no customer database. Amazon has tremendous details on its customers who purchase online, but it begins its transformation of Whole Foods with no historical customer information. Amazon is going to need to win over Whole Foods employees and help them adjust to a new way of making decisions".[4] A large amount of data will be needed to be collected in order to see if the store is generating enough interest from consumers to further pursue the creation of more physical stores and the advancement of Whole Foods. Amazon will need to improve their IT department and provide training courses to those employees and teams responsible for analyzing the data collected. There will be a two-week course geared toward showing and teaching the employees specific trends and how to analyze the needs, wants, and interests of their consumers regarding the future of their physical stores.

We feel that the answer to the question "how does one stay open to new discoveries and learning opportunities?" lies with both developers and investors when it comes to total success. Both must understand that they need to have the courage to admit that they do not know everything. For example, the construction industry tends to keep slow change of pace as architecture and materials change very gradually. In order to be innovative, leaders should be open to learning from other industries. It could even be from the IT industry, for example, the microservices architecture principles. In other words, it can be explained as a modular construction.

The honeycomb (as shown in Figure 6 below) is an ideal analogy for representing the evolutionary microservices architecture. Each cell in the honeycomb is not only independent but also integrated with other cells. By adding new cells, the honeycomb grows organically to a big, solid structure. When creating a new solution for customers and users the investment in the interdisciplinary team of engineers from different industries could be crucial. The more perspectives we have the more creative we are.

Honeycomb of modular/microservices architecture

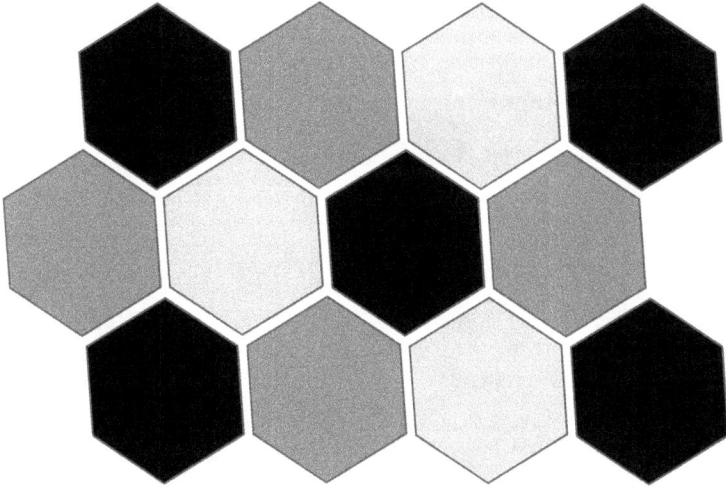

Raji Sivaraman and Michal Raczka 2017

Figure 6

Therefore, being courageous enough to learning what you realize you need more knowledge for and admitting the path is to grow more in specified areas to perform a project to the fullest details. This is *learning agility* in our minds. To analyze data better and more proficiently as the individuals and teams learn to rip apart information and analyze the vast amounts of data is a simple example here.

To have the learning agility honed, some of the remedies that can be employed are:

a) Be courageous to try, test, and be open for new learnings. Question everything.

b) It is ok to learn and fail. Failure is just the beginning. Failure creates new opportunities to learn.

c) Challenge the status quo in an attempt to make improvements.
d) When faced with something new, look for similarities between the situation and things you have done in the past. Draw on these similarities to frame the new challenge.
e) Make time to critically reflect on your past experiences.

"Leaders are never done learning and always seek to improve themselves. They are curious about new possibilities and act to explore them."[5]

Industry Applications by International Practitioners and Academia for Learning Agility

Agility is about learning and adapting which involves experimentation and adjusting the performance empirically to improve the results and impact. The curiosity to learn and improve continuously is the key for improving the outcomes. The learning capability helps in building a good knowledge base and allows better problem solving by evaluating different approaches to identify and decide the best approach.

Adaptability to enhance the skillsets in digital world will bring better results in dealing with uncertainty and technological changes. But at the same time measuring the business performance will radically shift from traditional or plan-driven approaches to empirical and evidence-based approaches. It's not only important to survive but to thrive in the world of uncertainty in order to gain the competitive advantage over others and to improve the quality of sustenance.

Gaurav Dhooper (PAL-I, *PMI-ACP*, *SAFe4*, *CSM*, *LSS-GB)*
Program Manager, RPA & Agile Practitioner at Genpact
INDIA

Our department has understood and acknowledge that we do not know everything and that we can do things better than we are currently doing. We understand that we should take advantage of all these opportunities and learn quickly with agility to design, plan, execute, manage and control our projects, using new technologies, methodologies, knowledge, etc., so that it will make our performance and in general our organization more competitive and efficient. The first step in the process will guide us in our new journey in the ocean of adaptation of our existing methodology in Engineering Design, Procurement, Project and Construction Management.

Rafael De La Rosa, Project-Portfolio Management Consultant,
PT. SMART tbk
INDONESIA / SPAIN

The data world is exploding with a multitude of tools, technologies and data trends requiring a culture of (constant) learning. Encouraging, and in some organizations, creating a culture where stakeholders and business users constantly seek to gain insight into what data is available, why strong data governance and analysis means, and more importantly, the ability to think forward about the key business outcomes they need to generate.

Patrick N Connally, Director, Teradata, Philadelphia,
USA

Some say we learn by our mistakes, some say there are no mistakes just lessons, and both are right. Some leaders say they forget their mistakes, but they never make them twice, while others continue to repeat them endlessly. In my company I advocate experimenting and learning from these experiments. I also say "Don't hide when an experiment fails and it becomes painful, this is your chance to relearn. Stop fearing failure, instead be open-minded. Because when you learn from these experiences whether they are successes or failures, you learn to recognise the signs and red flags in future settings. Adjusting via observation is an important quality". Finally, "failure" is only a thought construct, and it is nothing other than our subjective assessment of the reality which is what I have experienced in my company.

Joanna Staniszewska CEO, You'll Ltd.,
POLAND

Leading the way now is learning agility. In the new economy formal learning no longer plays a major role. The only way to survive the ever-changing environment is the readiness to learn and adapt. Accepting that you do not always know everything, having no fear of change and openness to learning are key.

Makheni Zonneveld, Future Readiness Coach,
NETHERLANDS

Even if it's the case when they meet, there is nothing new to say, they will say it anyway. Why? Because it is their actions that speak loudest, not their words.   In effect, what they are doing is demonstrating learning agility, they have curiosity and they discover fast what's working and what's not!

But when demonstrating personal agility and perhaps most importantly of all, when it comes to whether the chicken or the egg came first; they know that the philosophical question is not what came first, but what comes next

Paul Hodgkins, Executive Director, Paul Hodgkins Project Consultancy,
UNITED KINGDOM

Having the courage to understand that we are not good at everything is a good reflective practice. Understanding what you do not know leads to new discoveries and learning opportunities. Understanding peer perspectives helps change our assumptions thus opening our minds. A learning agile environment is what you want to create in a classroom and on a team.

Professor Linh Luong, Program Director of Master of Science in Project
Management, University of SEATTLE

"If you have different mindset, you will have a different outcome."

Jack Ma[1]

CHAPTER 8

---

organizational success

Outcomes Agility

achievement

Our goals and vision come to fruition when profits are realized sailing right alongside trust, partnership, and relationship. We strive for customer service and excellence, which are only truly measured by how the customer perceives the level of service or results. In the agile and burgeoning world of the corporate industry, many companies since their initial outset have confronted many issues. The range is too vast to epitomize. However, one can only imagine what it takes to be faced with callous challenges and figure out what to do next to better alleviate the circumstances and move toward a direction of diagnostic problem-solving.

Stephen Covey explains in his book *The 7 Habits of Highly Effective People*[2] that outputs always come last. In order to be successful, you need to start with the end in mind. This is all about vision. A project vision answers the question "why"—the essential starting point for inspiring action. A vision gives project participants a reason for contributing. It clarifies the project's purpose, eliminates confusion, unifies the team, and inspires them to do their best.

We need to understand the difference between output and outcome. It is not just the semantic[3] difference. We decided to have Outcomes Agility in our model because in the end it is all about the outcomes and impact that we create by our actions.

Outcomes are the benefit our customers receive from our work. This starts with truly understanding your customers' needs—their challenges, issues, constraints, priorities, etc. We can do this by applying the

Education Agility and walking in our customers' shoes in their neighborhoods, businesses, and cultures. "For many people, focusing on outcomes instead of outputs[4] requires a significant shift in culture and thinking. Defining outputs is easy, we're all focused on doing things. Doing something releases dopamine in our brain and makes us feel good. Doing things to achieve a certain outcome is a lot more complicated, and now success is not measured anymore by the percentage completion of our output."

Steve Denning[5] makes the distinction between output and outcome clear in his emphasis on the outcome of delighting our customers instead of just making more useful things.

Being resourceful takes projects to its highest performance. This involves being participative, affiliative, and transformational to obtain the highest form of outcomes. Outcomes agility is then certainly equated to the Agile Manifesto: "**Responding to Change Over Following a Plan.**" The metamorphosis of a butterfly is what outcomes agility symbolizes. Without the radical transformational changes, the butterfly cannot emerge into its varied colors and patterns if it were to follow a prescribed plan.

Nevertheless, this can happen if individuals conquer cognitive dissonance where they do not simultaneously hold two or more contradictory beliefs, ideas, or values. Opportunities to gain more knowledge, may it be an entrepreneur or not, excelling in your short- and long-term goals, and pushing for more is the story behind every successful organization. Performance will be at its intended height and maybe more by keeping all of the above agilities in operation at the peak level and for nearly all entities. Whether it is for nonprofit or for profit this operational endowment if kept at a steady pace, any aspiration can be achieved.

The seven agilities are so closely attuned to cognitive dissonance. The reason is because this will reflect positivity on the overall performance of the company because it provides support and an understanding, especially in scenarios such as acquisitions and mergers. Sometimes evolving endowment within a business and training teams for improvement are idyllic methods to get the individuals ready for what is yet to come. It is frequently quicker and further operational to endorse from the internal rankings instead of exploring innovative endowment outside of the company.

Formal outcome studies that Daniel Amen[6] does are synonymous to Outcomes Agility. He says you learn more when you look more, hard and with intent. In his psychiatry world, it is to look at an image of a brain to solve problems. In our model it is to look at oneself and the personal attributes that will enhance an organization and the teams that shape and construct the organization.

Finally if an organization aspires to go full blast to achieve and reach their intended shores with outcomes that surpass their intentions, outcomes agility is certainly the steering wheel that can be used as the tool.

There is no straight line between vision and outcomes as shown in Figure 7 below. We need to remember about additional ingredients like strategy formulation, execution, and continuous improvement to make our outcomes better.

Vision Outcomes Cycle

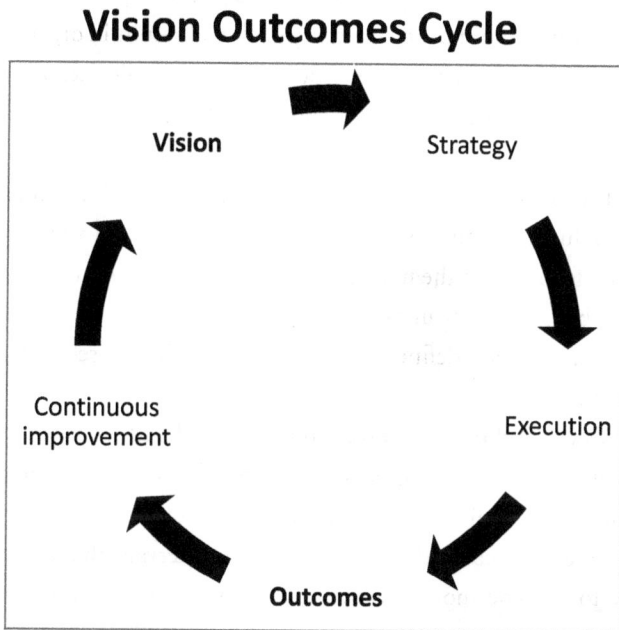

Raji Sivaraman and Michal Raczka 2020

Figure 7

Vision is supported by the Personal Agility Lighthouse (PALH™) model as an essential starting point for inspiring action.

Strategy formulation can be very well supported by the "Brightline Initiative's 10 Guiding Principles."

Combining the PALH™ model principles and the 10 guiding principles will help leaders shrink the costly and wasteful gap between strategy design and delivery.

"Practices can change, business models are disrupted, technology evolves, but principles do not change. They are the soul of strategy design and delivery."[7]

Execution needs to be done through action and feedback in short cycles. Project Portfolio Management supported by Quarterly Business Reviews (QBR)[8] and Objective and Key Result (OKR) can help leaders execute, measure, and deliver outcomes for customers. The QBR is a planning ceremony that links the business strategy with the quarterly planning. It is a continuous process often used by Spotify, ING, and other big and small companies.

OKR[9] is a popular, best practice strategic planning process for setting, communicating, and tracking quarterly goals and results in organizations. OKRs are a simple way to create structure for companies, teams, and individuals. The secret sauce when it comes to OKRs is to make them very ambitious (vision and strategy driven). That way OKRs enable individuals and teams to focus on the bigger picture and to achieve more than they thought they would. OKRs encourage a result- and value-oriented culture by focusing on the main priorities. It also increases the autonomy level and boosts self-organization. What is the difference between KPIs and OKRs? KPIs are defined by a manager, OKRs are self-chosen and self-driven.

It is essential during the execution to have closed feedback loops to continuously improve our approach to better outcomes. Drawing similes from the Agile Manifesto,[10] it has the concept of continuous improvement as one of its core principles: "At regular intervals, the team reflects on how to become more effective, then tunes and adjusts its behavior accordingly."

Continually reviewing our efforts and strategy execution generally encourages incremental improvement over time. Improvements are based on many small changes rather than the radical changes that might arise from large research and development initiatives.[11]

On quarterly basis we review the outcomes, we adopt and adapt to changes, we revise our vision, and continue with execution of strategy.

To have the outcomes agility honed, some of the remedies that can be employed are:

a) Define your vision, define outcomes for your customers and business partners. Delight them.
b) Move from long-term goals to a continuous-state-of-achieving.
c) Seek feedback, benchmark yourself.
d) Measure, measure, measure!
e) Stretch your limits—believe in yourself.

Industry Applications by International Practitioners and Academia for Outcomes Agility

They say that you will never be happy if you are always striving for excellence. In my opinion as the head of my company, 'having done something is better than something excellent which will never be done'. However, I think that it is impossible to achieve anything if we do not push ourselves to get the best out of ourselves. It is easy. Do you want to develop? Always be a step ahead of your comfort zone and keep improving. Clients will appreciate if the agency has its own quality check internally. The whole team can be engaged to improve the project only when the company culture is supporting and promoting these behaviors. For example, in my company I allow the proper time for the project delivery, not always agreeing with the deadlines given by clients enabling better outcomes.

Joanna Staniszewska CEO, You'll Ltd.,
POLAND

Everything comes to an end, which could mean the beginning of something new and unknown. Outcomes Agility, can help our industry to be more enterprising, inspiring and push us to seek our limits, not settle for mundane bureaucratic work and salary. We know and believe that we can do better, it is a question that, both on a personal and group level, we should answer by giving the best we have and strive to continue growing together, supporting each other. The benefit is that almost everything we want to challenge has the potential to start a flywheel. Once it gets spinning, it can spin faster within more context control.

Rafael De La Rosa, Project-Portfolio Management Consultant,
PT. SMART tbk
INDONESIA / SPAIN

A recognition that unless you know what outcomes you seek, there is little point in seeking the outcomes! They also recognize just as the winds can change direction, so can the outcomes they seek. Having an outcomes agility through the portfolio of projects means sometimes the winds will be at your back, and at other times, are trying to knock you off your feet;

but either way, accountability for staying on your feet, or being knocked to the ground, is always clear and undisputable.

Paul Hodgkins, Executive Director, Paul Hodgkins Project Consultancy,
UNITED KINGDOM

In the world of higher education, "outcomes" are a big deal. Ultimately, we want to make sure that students are learning what we think they need to learn in order to be successful in the real world. Outcomes can be as micro in the course level as well as macro at the university level. It becomes a guiding principle on what we need to teach our students and how we go about it. We assess at differing levels in order to determine whether a student is really "learning". This is critical for determining transformational action steps needed in order to reach the outcome or goal.

Professor Linh Luong, Program Director of Master of Science in Project
Management, University of SEATTLE

What is the roadmap for your data, and what is your end state? Nothing could be more critical than focusing on the outcome of the story you want to tell. Identifying and generating genuine and sustainable data insights requires leaders to clearly articulate goals, and an attitude of continuous improvement. These attitudes, and the engagement strategies required to sustain them, are pivotal for effective data transformation. Times like this, the old adage 'if you don't know where you're going, any road will get you there' rings true. Clearly defining your organizational vision, roadmap, and targeted goals requires visionary leaders and inspired constituents.

Driving successful data transformation requires intentionality. The journey leans on leaders to master more than just a mastery of data and analytics. Driving change and transformation through data analytics require an agile mindset. Leveraging the seven agility dimensions offers the opportunity to effectuate and propagate change and maximize the impact of data and analytics.

Patrick N Connally, Director, Teradata, Philadelphia,
USA

Outcomes agility inspires you to constantly better yourself to excel to the next level and constantly strive for better outcomes in any venture.

With the help of the PALH™ method, the people who invested in this project would have started with asking the right questions with the desired outcome in mind. Their desired outcome was to have an impact on the environment by collecting good recyclable plastic but they invested in equipment that separates different materials perfectly. The solution is to ask the right questions like; what problem does equipment X solve?

Makheni Zonneveld, Future Readiness Coach,
NETHERLANDS

In order to maximize the value creation for the customer, one must focus on outcomes and impact. For instance, measuring the business performance in terms of ability to innovate includes the trends of defects reported in software delivery. If the number of code review and functionality defects are decreasing sprint over sprint it shows better ability of the team to innovate. Similarly, reducing the technical debt over time will improve and bring excellence in the delivery. One of the important values of Scrum requires commitment by the team for achieving the Sprint goal as the Sprint events are time-boxed.

In essence organizational agility can be better achieved through honing personal agility using the Personal Agility Light House (PALH™) Model- "a segway through adaptability", agile mindset, growth mindset, business agility, continuous delivery predictability, empiricism, business value delivery, thus achieving ultimate organizational performance.

Gaurav Dhooper (PAL-I°, PMI-ACP°, SAFe4°, CSM°, LSS-GB)
Program Manager, RPA & Agile Practitioner at Genpact,
INDIA

"Discipline is the bridge between goals and accomplishment."

Jim Rohn[1]

CHAPTER 9

The Eighth Flavor— Discipline

The importance of Personal Agility

We have all of these formal theories, exams, workshops, and everything that is process oriented with tools and methodologies for the word "agility." But guess what, if the agile mindset is not inherent in a person, life can be quite a challenge. A simple example, from a mariner's life. When they travel across longitudes, every 15 degrees is a one-hour change in the clocks that we need to do. Everyone complains about daylight savings in countries that change the clocks for just one hour twice a year. Imagine doing it multiple times a day and then doing this as and when the course of the ship changes. It takes a humungous toll on a human body and mind. So all of the 7 agilities come into play. Therefore, the importance of being agile should strike a chord very early in an individual and organization.

Agile is widely used by many industries. In order to have a successful agile environment, we need to deal with cultural changes and we also need something called the "Agile Mindset." People with highly honed Personal Agility can create enhanced Organizational Agility. There are many people who are focused on organizations, but forget about individuals. Focusing on individuals who can and want to change organizations is quintessential for the success of a project or the organization.

When the direction of the wind changes, the remedies to overcome the changes should not lose the focus of the goals of the organization. This can happen only when each individual hones one's personal agility skills. Joseph M Juran, a management consultant, took Vilfredo Pareto's theory and applied Pareto analysis to many applicable areas. It is based on the idea that 80% of problems are traced to 20% of the causes.[2]

When we apply Pareto analysis to our PALH^{TM} model, it takes into consideration the capacity, alternatives, and capability of an individual. Maybe the 20% of causes is to hone personal agility. Figure 8 (Organizational Complexities) below explains an organizational viewpoint from the personal agility angle. Recognizing unsuccessful efforts to progress and common dysfunctions of an individual will aid toward an effective approach to boost organizational performance. The strengths and weakness of an individual defining dynamism, criticality, visibility, and functionality culminate in tailoring individual practices to become sustainable in the long run.

Organizational Complexities

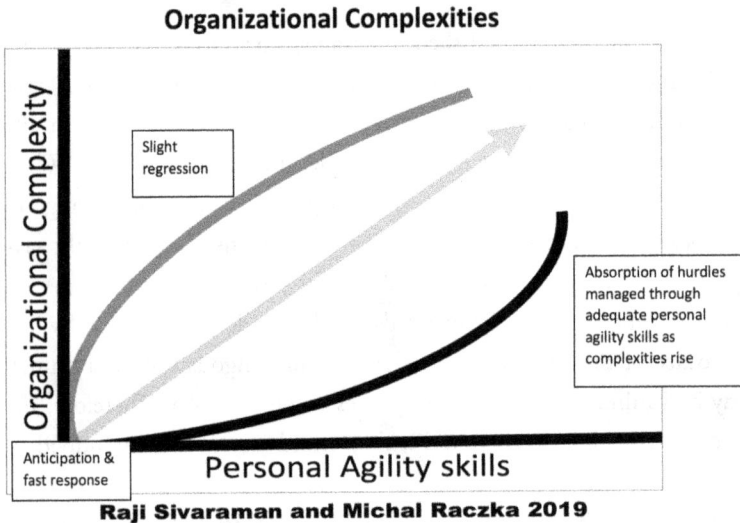

Raji Sivaraman and Michal Raczka 2019

Figure 8

A simple example of complexities in organizations is what is shown in Figure 8 above.

The ideal scenario is to staff up each time there is an increase in organizational complexity with competent persons who have very highly honed personal agility skills. In Figure 8 above depicted by the **"straight line,"** the department has the availability of competent persons and costs are unconstrained. So there is no advanced planning in staffing and qualified personnel can be added to advantage as and when needed. Or every individual has his/her personal agility honed with all seven agilities.

In the real world, the above is not always true. There are constraints in terms of competency, availability, costs that need to be budgeted or absolutely no finance available, and so on and so forth.

The **"black curve"** represents the situation where the organization has done advanced planning of the oncoming organizational complexity, budgeted in anticipation and thought ahead of capacity building pro-actively. So, in the early part of the complexity realization, capability is adequately absorbed. The organization predicts and has anticipated the needed personal agility skills to be mobilized to address the organizational complexities early and head-on with training, pairing, switching shoes, and numerous other means. The organization, with the momentum gained, stays ahead of the curve. The consequential benefit is that it gains the competency of scenario building as it has the capacity (redundancy) to engage in such forward thinking exercises.

The **"dark gray curve"** represents the situation where there is lack of advanced planning in the organization in anticipation of the on-coming organizational complexity. Early detection of wants and re-quirements of personal agility skills is not done proactively. This could be due to lack of visibility of needs, lack of resources, or the need that is not budgeted and as such has to go through a long approval pro-cess and many other reasons. When the multiple levels of complexity situation hit the organization, there are no competent resources, with the right skills, to professionally address the circumstances at hand. So there is a slight regression (neglected reaction, so to speak) before an ad hoc team with perceived personal agility skills is put together to address the issues at hand or intense training, etc., is provided to name a few recourses. Upon realization of the state of affairs, an organized reaction/drill takes place to address the conditions on hand. This is re-actionary and is hard to catch up and be ahead of the curve, while the complexities grow in parallel.

Are we born with personal agility or is this something we can learn?

While some of them can be natural for individuals—we can say are born with them, others can be mastered and honed.

A simple example—it is synonymous to health and fitness in a gym catering for different people in a totally different manner by a trainer even though everyone needs it. There is no competition here, neither is it a constant. At any given point in your life the 7 agilities change. It is important to keep them in balance.

One of the myths that should be debunked is that agility is for everyone. In our opinion, it is not. There are different agilities and not all are for everybody. Maybe having just two of them is perfect in your situation. Though it does not mean that you shouldn't strive for more. Keeping them in balance should be the goal.

This is one of the reasons we have created the Personal Agility Index. This is a *self-analysis assessment* (see Appendix) exercise where every participant in our workshops can learn more about himself/herself to find out which agilities are already honed and which should be further developed. Then you are provided with hints/tools, etc., on how to learn to hone them. So it is a mix and match. The PALH™ *self-analysis assessment* (see Appendix) is not something that we brand you for life. Each time you take it the results will change. This is because we change as we grow, get more experienced as we work, study, and interact, etc.

Not all seven needs to be honed by all the organizations or individuals. It depends on the industry, the individual, situation, etc. That is why we use an individualized approach versus a standard approach. We deploy a very unique and structured method to refine one's personal agility to hone organizational agility to its optimum level.

Personal Agility is about individuals and the goal is to build better organizations. Personal Agility is about how an individual with his/her mindset, culture, and personal agility can influence organizations to become more successful. Anyone or any organization that needs to want the clarity, collaborative working environments with relationships, basically those who want to want to, if that makes sense. Sometimes you have no choice.

Do not Measure what you do not Use or Need

In Chapter 1, we spoke about "what you measure is what you get" (WYMIWYG). If we were to use all of the seven agilities of the model, there are examples where there are many resources used unnecessarily sometimes. Time expended, cost overruns, and many more superfluous items are directed toward projects that need not be measured. This is because some teams in the organization's utilization hours at that given time are for that particular project or for a certain client.

It is just as Jim Whitehurst, President and CEO of Red Hat, says in his *Harvard Business Review* article[3]: "But what about the kinds of jobs where measuring someone's 'output' isn't about counting the number of widgets they produced, but rather it's about how they managed a team or influenced others or helped people collaborate better? While it might be easy to measure someone's output on an assembly line, how do we decide how well a manager manages or a leader leads?"

As Figure 9 below shows, we have to make sure that the need is justified to start the measuring. Then when the actual measuring is carried out, the needs of the measurement as well as the initiative are to be accurately and appropriately taken into account and catered for.

Need Justified Measurements

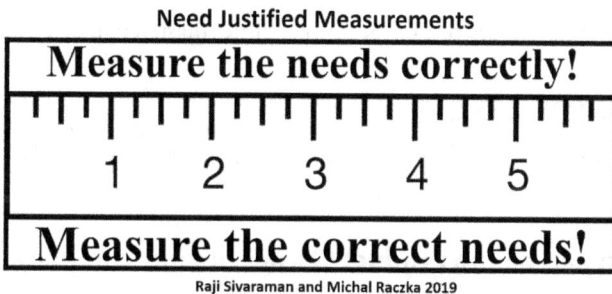

| **Measure the needs correctly!** |
| **1   2   3   4   5** |
| **Measure the correct needs!** |

Raji Sivaraman and Michal Raczka 2019

Figure 9

Can Personal Agility and Scrum Be Yin and Yang?

Honing the PALH™ model can be a complex and adaptive challenge for an individual. As we sail through the voyage of the PALH™ model, we now explain how we can reach the lighthouse. This entails one to choose the vital agilities/flavors. As explained earlier, measurements are important as well for which there needs to be methods, tools, etc.[4] Let's take scrum for instance, as this framework is the most widely used around the world.

According to scrum.org, scrum is a framework within which people can address complex adaptive problems, while productively and creatively delivering products of the highest possible value. The PALH™ model is built on seven flavors. It comprises of Learning, Cerebral, Emotional, Education, Change, Political, and Outcomes Agility. If we explore the subtleties of getting the organizational outcome through these skill sets and tie it to each of the agility, we find that the scrum values have a great fit into these. Scrum is for predictability, meaning knowing what to expect, and reliability, meaning commitments by oneself to deliver appropriately toward an organization's lighthouse.

Scrum framework as a discipline is the goal for mastering all of the seven agilities. One needs to have a certain amount of discipline. The dictionary meaning of discipline is "to train oneself to do something in a controlled and habitual way." Discipline also means "it is an activity or experience that provides training." Honing your Personal Agility will help ease working with the scrum framework on a personal level. To give just a few examples, the three roles of Scrum are the Product Owner, Scrum Master, and the Development Team Member. All of them have definitely the need to have every one of the seven agilities mastered to deliver success.

Example 1. Product Owner

You are the Product Owner of your personal agility journey!

You can be the Product Owner of your company agility journey!

The product owner takes the lead in many areas of product development, which would involve a host of agile thinking and mindsets to produce a product that caters for all the business requirements. They are required to use their deep wealth of multiple knowledge to stage-manage and put forth their visualization to a number of stakeholders. They may also be in need to help the team meet their objectives during a sprint. This is where the *Education Agility* brings about wearing the hat of another to feel the pain points so as to get the work done in a manner that is satisfactory to all stakeholders.

Example 2. Scrum Master

The benefit of using the PALH™ model is discovering what your influence as a Scrum Master is and how the Scrum Master can improve and mature. Therefore, this model benefits the Scrum Master who is responsible for the scrum process and/or discipline. Here is a simple example:

Cerebral Agility and *Political Agility* are two flavors that will empower a Scrum Master. This is because the Scrum Master has to constantly be putting into place practices that can help the team jump hurdles. To break through an organizational bottleneck, link dependencies with ease, and work through constraints is just one high-level role of the Scrum Master.

In your personal journey you need to keep your goals and you need to guard your personal discipline. You need to play the role of a Scrum Master and use education agility.

Example 3. Development Team Member

Mckinsey says: "The two most important factors for a person working in an agile environment are the ability to handle ambiguity and a high level of agreeableness."[5]

Scrum Development Team consists of professionals who do the work of delivering a potentially releasable product at the end of each sprint. Only members of the Development Team create the increment. Development teams are structured and empowered by the organization to organize and manage their own work. Team members in order to create the increment need to hone *Learning Agility* and *Change Agility*.

In your personal journey the increment can be an improvement of your PALH™ index or real-life application of one of the examples we provide in this book.

In essence, a development team member is "committed" as opposed to the others like the users, resource managers, and various other external and internal stakeholders who are only "involved." Therefore, it is paramount for the team member to hone all seven agilities for the success of an organization as each member is responsible for all the work that is to be done.

Just as in a daily scrum the "3 whats'" are discussed:

- what was completed,
- what work is being done now,
- what the impediments are;

for each team member the seven agilities of the model need to be deeply imbedded for the team/vertical/department/organization to sail the seas unshaken.

Yin Yang – PALH™ and Scrum

Raji Sivaraman and Michal Raczka 2018

Figure 10

Ancient Chinese people were greatly interested in the relationships of two components that explained the logic that existed between each other called the Yin Yang.[6] Drawing this analogy, Yin Yang for Personal Agility and Scrum, the inference is that in order to hone Personal Agility we may need to achieve personal discipline through Scrum as shown in Figure 10 above.

The deduction therefore is simply an extrapolation of the five Scrum values given below.[7] The seven agilities go in tandem with the scrum values as connected below per the Yin Yang correlation.

Scrum values riding alongside the seven agilities

Courage—Learning Agility, for example: admitting that you don't know everything is a courageous act to stop failure from occurring.

Commitment—Outcomes Agility, for example: working toward the vision, mission, and the goals of the organization navigating through the waves and storms that hit you along your way.

Focus—Change Agility, for example: where the Last Responsible Moment (LRM) comes into play and Cerebral Agility, for example, where focusing on the task at hand like wearing a horse's blinders to prevent running off course.

Openness—Here Political Agility lends its glorious virtue to achieve organizational agility.

Respect—This value is a savior to the work at hand when it comes to Emotional Agility and Educational Agility. This would be right in place here to empathize and respect the pain points of the person sitting next to you at work or your contemporary at any level.

Honing personal agility is to keep discovering and keep exploring the strategies to achieve better organizational outcomes through individual skill sets. We discover that our principles that we spoke about in the introduction map very well to the scrum values and our seven agilities map to the principles.

Education agility
- constantly keep advancing ourselves to reroute our capabilities

Change agility
- relearn ourselves to improve competencies

Emotional agility
- treat others with deference

Political agility
- transparency for organizational growth

Cerebral agility
- focus on organizational goals not the impediments of alterations

Learning agility

- ○ have the courage to say "I don't know"

Outcomes agility

- ○ commit to excel in the outcome that is foreseen

All of the above scrum values will certainly lead to successful out-comes of any given project. Thus honing the seven agilities to enhance *Organizational Agility*, and coming ashore with groomed *Outcomes Agility* in any project, program, or portfolio management arena.

"Success today requires the agility and drive to constantly rethink, reinvigorate, react, and reinvent."

Bill Gates[1]

CHAPTER 10

Put on the Captain's Resilience Hat

We ponder about the approach to reach the shores. Performance impact of any organization, be it small, medium, large, or mega, depends a lot on the team members, the managers, vendors, suppliers, sponsors, and many more.

To hone the seven agilities to an optimum level, we feel that the winds that bring you to the safe shores are the qualities of:

- listening,
- promoting group thinking,
- hearing without interruption,
- being aware of one's surroundings,
- environment on the *first level*.

As part of our research, we have come across many similarities of our inference with many industries. One such is the American Institute of Aeronautics and Astronautics article[2] "Agile Development Methods for Space Operations." Their conclusion is that Agile has more benefits over traditional methods since the process is iterative, continuous, and integrated. The result is a more productive and effective team and product.

As a Proof of concept (PoC) of the model, Marguerita Cheng, CEO of Blue Ocean Global Wealth, Washington, D.C., USA, says: Bringing It All Together to reach the Personal Agility Lighthouse (PALH™) safely: "There is a confluence of factors that prompt the need to be agile (pause and pivot) to stay relevant. All of these macro trends mean that our profession has to be agile and think of different ways to deliver advice. Financial planning is about controlling spending, managing credit, reducing taxes, increasing savings, protecting family and assets, and building wealth for the future.

This process entails gathering financial information, establishing life goals, evaluating a client's current financial status, and developing a strategy to help them achieve their life goals. An exceptional financial advisor is a master of the seven pillars of PALH™ model who can readily identify his or her clients' needs and provide them with exceptional service and advice that takes into account a rapidly changing financial landscape."

To read more about Marguerita Cheng's article, please visit http://agilitydiscoveries.com/articles/ or https://www.iris.xyz/contributor/raji-and-michal

Personal Agility happens at the leadership level as well as at the individual level. It is all about mindsets and attitudes of leaders mostly. Although it is easy to understand, it is very difficult to implement and master. **Personal Agility** always works at some level. This level can be tested and checked against one's ability through the PALH™ Index, a reflection and contemplation valuation tool where leaders and individuals can learn more about himself/herself. There is very slim chance of it not working. However, not every project in an organization gets done the same way. There is also the unexpected. Individuals react in different ways for different storms that hit them unanticipated. This model works when:

- The more agile and lean the environment is, the easier it is to use the model.
- The model itself will improve the agility environment anyway.

Application of Personal Agility to the Agile World

Personal Agility naturally applies to the agile world and to an agile organization. This is a perfect fit where people and the personal agility flavors are consistent with the agile culture.

Build your backbone culture with Personal Agility!

Leaders who strive for excellence and high levels of project performance are able to achieve better outcomes by following the Agile Manifesto values and the seven agilities. These need to be propagated throughout the whole organization and not be confined only to the delivery streams.

Executives and teams can build an agile culture. Progress can be measured by using the seven agilities as well as the PALH™ Index, a self-analysis (see Appendix) tool to gauge and hone the weaker which are below par flavors of an individual. Such organizations are able to achieve a high agility stage where project performance drives value and tremendous outcomes.

Figure 11 below is our explanation and adaptation of project performance indicators taken from a white paper about organizational agility from the Project Management Institute.[3] It shows how success is impacted by a high agility stage. The average percentage of projects completed on time, on budget, achieving business objectives and forecasted Return on Investment (ROI) is significantly greater in organizations reporting high agility than those reporting low agility.

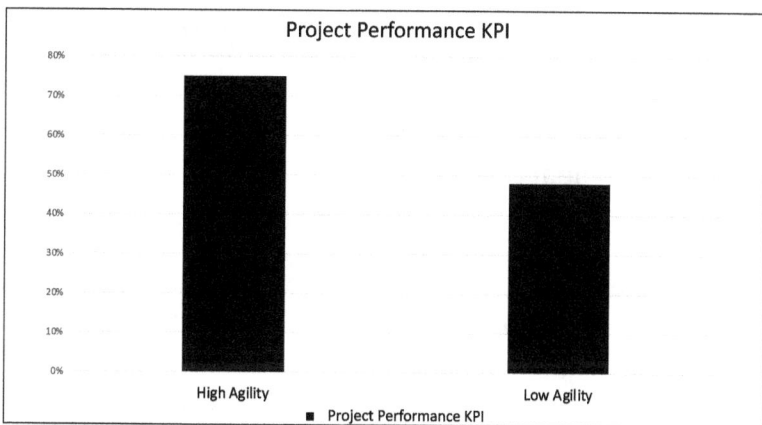

Source: Adapted from Organizational Agility: Where Speed Meets Strategy (2012)

Figure 11

Application of the Personal Agility to the Waterfall World

Personal Agility does not normally apply in the waterfall world. People who are guided by the seven agilities can feel some frictions when experiencing the waterfall culture. There are two choices then. Either they will move to another organization or they will change the organization they are in now. Many times, these people and leaders who have a high PALH™ Index (see Appendix) lead the transformation of organizations toward agility. When the level of frictions becomes too high they start looking for opportunities outside of the company. It is very important in every organization to recognize the team members who have such a mindset and high PALH™ Index (see Appendix). Executives who aim for high agility can follow the PALH™ model and apply it at an individual level in order to prepare future leaders who will transform the organization into the agile world.

<u>Our Perspective:</u>

We can see a lot of organizations where product/project teams are agile and upper management is waterfall.

We have never seen an organization where upper management is agile and product/project teams are waterfall.

Personal Agility helps to make upper management and product/project teams agile.

Therefore, the inference and deduction that we have landed upon is that the Personal Agility works better in the agile world as individual's values and the organization's culture lead to high levels of project performance. At the same time waterfall organizations can be treated as a challenge for individuals who achieved a high level of PALH™ Index (see Appendix). These people usually become leaders who are responsible for game-changing transformations. Individuals with a high Index in the agile world are able to deliver maximum project performance. Individuals with a high Index in the waterfall world can either drive an organization toward high project performance and have the opportunity to create a new culture or they naturally move to organizations that are already in the agile world. From our perspective and research, it is very uncommon to be in the middle.

The most important and noteworthy item for healthy organizations is to recognize, adapt, and adopt the Index, measure it and apply to any project, program, or portfolio in their organization. This would bring out the optimum results in our opinion. Summing up and reaching the shore with the seven agilities guiding the light with the navigational aid of the Index, the higher the level of the Index, the higher the level of project performance that can be achieved.

On a *second level*, focus and thinking outside the box automatically bring forth self-worth and compassion for others. To arrive ashore smoothly we take the four values from the Agile Manifesto and look at them though the seven agilities binoculars. The agilities that show their guiding light to the safe shores are:

1. Individuals and Interactions Over Processes and Tools
   The agilities that would fit this statement are ***Political Agility and Emotional Agility***. If processes and tools are seen as the way to manage product development and everything associated with it, people and the way they approach the work must conform to the processes and tools.[4] If an individual is permitted to contribute their own exclusive values to a project, the results turn out to be invariably quite potent. This then is an agile environment, which is human-centric and quite readily explosive as with any situation where people are in the right, left, and everywhere. Therefore, even though valuing processes and tools have benefits, civil communications and behavior, where no politics and emotions run high, realize greater benefits for a project if you value individuals and interactions highly.

2. Working Software Over Comprehensive Documentation
   For this value, we feel that ***Learning Agility*** and ***Cerebral Agility*** fit in perfectly. In a *Journal of Software Engineering Research and Development* article relating to this value of the agile manifesto, the authors say, "agile teams impose governance on their own activities"[5] for this agile manifesto value. This most certainly means that no matter how much of documentation one has, when there is a crisis situation, one has to be bold enough to say "I don't know" (learning agility). Going beyond the documentation to come up with a ready and apt solution (cerebral agility) to make things work the way it is intended to be; will save the day.

3. Customer Collaboration Over Contract Negotiation

   Education Agility seems to weave right into this value. This is a true reflection of the sentence in the summary of the paper titled "The Relationship between Customer Collaboration and Software Project Overruns." The main finding was that good collaboration with customers, facilitated by frequent communication, was associated with projects that experienced a lesser magnitude of effort overruns.[6] In essence what this means is that education agility in our model refers to empathy applied directly to the understanding and comprehending of the customer's thought process, and further needs. The real value in being empathetic and honing one's education agility is to make sure that the customers' mindset is what the collaboration should be directed toward. Once the inner wants of the customer are securely captured, contracts can then be negotiated congenially for which one needs to educate oneself to find these nuances through the workings of the customer.

4. Responding to Change Over Following a Plan

   Change Agility and *Outcomes Agility* are where we find this value to be intertwining. In an article written by Cecil Williams and David Kessler, August 19, 2013, "No amount of thinking can replace hands-on experience with the real system"[7] is a true testimony to this value. For the outcome of any endeavor to be at its peak, the real problems and changes happen during the execution. As such when one follows the plan in its entirety and not use change agility in the execution, there is bound to be rework, re-budgeting, and much more as injection of changes is inevitable in any space. Therefore, honing the outcomes agility to its desired height, the fourth agile manifesto value is of paramount significance.

To wrap it up from the individual to the corporate journey standpoint, as Figure 12 on the next page shows the cruise from *Personal Agility* to *Organizational Agility*,[8] the seven agilities serve as the lighthouse to reach the peak of the project performance for any entity.

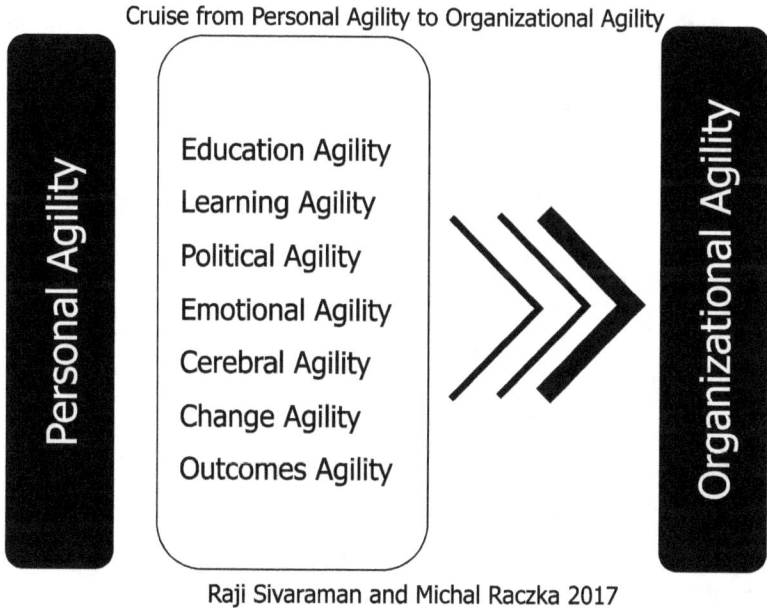

Cruise from Personal Agility to Organizational Agility

Personal Agility

Education Agility
Learning Agility
Political Agility
Emotional Agility
Cerebral Agility
Change Agility
Outcomes Agility

Organizational Agility

Raji Sivaraman and Michal Raczka 2017

Figure 12

Personal Agility cannot be considered as a homeless island. It must be treated as a quintessential ingredient that should be supported by business domain skills and experiences. It should also not be confined to select teams, departments, verticals, or team members only. To improve organizational performance further it is advisable that all stakeholders master Personal Agility. Introspection is one way to conduct continuous self-improvement. This means asking oneself, what am I doing now and where is the path to improve myself. Once a path is found, retrospection follows to decide what to do next. The transformation of oneself geared toward the organization is profound when the introspection/retrospection circle is complete.

Analogies of the PALH™ model can be drawn from far, wide, and multidimensional spaces. To vet the appetite of the readers of this book, let's take a peek at the eight practices of enlightenment in Buddhism. The 8-fold factors of Buddha[9] have great applications to all of the seven agilities in our model. Talking about who our model benefits, it is for those who want to make a better organization be more successful just as these factors portray. To extrapolate a few of the 8-fold factors:

Right View. The right way to think about life is to see the world through the eyes of wisdom and compassion is what Buddha says. *Change Agility in our minds is exactly that—to change per the situation and be wise and compassionate as you ride the change.*

Right Thought. We are what we think. Clear and kind thoughts build good, strong characters, says Buddha. *Cerebral Agility* in our model is to think clearly even at a moment of dire stress or pressure.

Right Conduct. No matter what we say, others know us from the way we behave. Before we criticize others, we should first see what we do ourselves. *Political Agility* is right on target here where we do an introspection to hone this agility.

Right Effort. A worthwhile life means doing our best at all times. This is *Education agility* in our model which is to keep one's acumen sharp to do the best in all kinds of scenarios. This hold true even when one has to put on the shoes of another to pick up the pace of the work to make a bad situation end successfully.

Right Mindfulness. This means being aware of our thoughts, words, and deeds. *Emotional Agility in our model is what is portrayed here, where all of these come into play. This needs innovative handling to avoid collision and destruction of the organization as well as the employees.*

Right Concentration. Focus on one thought or object at a time. *Learning and being focused on the right mindset to want to learn more and to acknowledge that one does not know everything is synonymous to Learning Agility in our model.*

All of the above brings forth *Outcomes Agility* in any organization no matter what the industry is or in which arena or space or geography!

"When I do something, it is all about self-discovery. I want to learn and discover my own limits."

Larry Ellison[1]

CHAPTER 11

The Personal Agility Lighthouse™ Brings Us Safely to the Shores

As the ropes are moored and the ship is berthed, so is our journey of the Personal Agility Lighthouse being tied and fastened fully equipped, secured, and honed with the seven agilities skills.

Thomas Martin, CEO, Forward Intelligence Group, Singapore/ Philippines/Germany, in his article, "Driving business agility with portfolio management," sums it all up beautifully with the following questions:

1. *Educational Agility*: Do we have an open mind and are we listening properly?
2. *Change Agility*: Are we realistic about what we can achieve with our current resources in the current situation?
3. *Political Agility*: Do we understand what is going on in the external environment?
4. *Emotional Agility*: Are we taking charge of our moods, thoughts, and behaviors?
5. *Cerebral Agility*: Do we respond quickly and powerfully enough to the challenges we face?
6. *Learning Agility*: What are our capabilities and resources?
7. *Outcomes Agility*: Are we producing the results we want and are the results we are producing sustainable in the long term?

Thomas Martin further writes that: "People who understand what 'agile' means for them, are more likely to support an agile transformation. Investing in people agility is an effective bottom-up measure that complements portfolio management and an agile transformation particularly well. It has a wide organizational reach and can be executed independently.

An organization that asks and answers these questions regularly is on a good track. It will remain agile and be seen as responsive to change. The Personal Agility Lighthouse™ (PALH™) model created by the founders of AgilityDiscoveries facilitates the speed and change to achieve continuous competitive advantage in serving the organization and its multiple stakeholders."

The entire article of Thomas Martin can be found at http://agilitydiscoveries.com/articles/ and https://www.iris.xyz/contributor/raji-and-michal

According to Wikipedia, intelligence has been defined in many ways: the capacity for logic, understanding, self-awareness, learning, emotional knowledge, reasoning, planning, creativity, critical thinking, and problem-solving.[2] All of this collectively is precisely what our PALH™ model stands for: to hone the outcomes agility using all of the other 6 agilities. When many individuals put together each of their intelligence toward a common goal, it becomes collective intelligence. Social aggregation is found in ants, bees, birds, etc., as they individually contribute to their own perspective project such as their nest, hives, and flying pattern. Similarly, different representations and interpretations of the power and meaning of lighthouses in real life and projects also have subtle differences. But they all serve the same purpose—guiding everyone to safe shores. We at AgilityDiscoveries using the same analogy guide projects, project managers, and organizations from Personal Agility to Organizational Agility. It does not matter what tools and methodologies are used by each lighthouse to guide everyone toward land roughing all of the storms and winds. The outcome and vision is the same, to gain what you intended to achieve!

At the end of the day, nothing should be done for optics. Personal agility is about what one believes in. We went over very thoroughly the "whys" for the bumpy ride of the transformations in the agile/digital paradigm shift. McKinsey's Aaron De Smet and Chris Gagnon[3] explain what is driving organizational agility, why it matters, and what to do in their article "Going from fragile to agile." They talk about value, integrity, collaboration, and excellence. All of these are true indicators for convergence of markets as is a well-designed personal agility that needs to flow through to organizational agility. Therefore, if you want to make any kind of transformation in your company it is a good idea to reach a state of organizational agility and this can be made possible through the honing of the seven Personal Agility models at all levels. Balancing all of the seven agilities will give *Outcomes Agility* that aids a good organization to sail smoothly.

Interdisciplinary teams use different perspectives and this guides them to convergent and creative options. To quote an example of a Project Manager (PM), it is important for PMs to wear two hats:

- Leader of a team—Leadership from the PMI Talent Triangle (shown below from the Project Management Institute). These skills help us develop a vision for our team members and inspire them to achieve the target. Leadership is about winning as a team, not as an individual.
- Partner to a business—Strategic and Business Management from PMI Talent Triangle (shown below from the Project Management Institute). These skills help us analyze business decisions before you implement them. These analyses include cost benefit analysis, strength and weakness analysis, market conditions, legal requirements, and compliance, etc.

The PMI Talent Triangle®

Putting on the captain's hat of resilience (explained in depth in Chapter 10), a PM seeks to be a leader and partner by wanting to know/ learn/read more, be more curious about project outcomes, team members, organizational strategy, to list a few guidelines.

In conclusion, competitive advantages are always in the back of a business's mind. Typically, people that work with aspiration and have a strong relationship with their business are the individuals who push for improvement, can handle more inventiveness, deliver greater value of work, and keep the corporation thriving. Performance peaks at this level when all of the seven agilities are at their peak. In divergence, disengaged individuals and teams are unfavorable for the establishment's image since they can fraudulently steer the other individuals in the cluster with debauched elucidations. Moreover, the fact that it decelerates competence can prompt core members of the team to look for new horizons. Recognizing these kinds of personnel and dealing with the cause of their unhappiness is very essential.

This is why we at AgilityDiscoveries have come up with our PALH™ model and would like to wish every reader happy sailings to your desired shores!

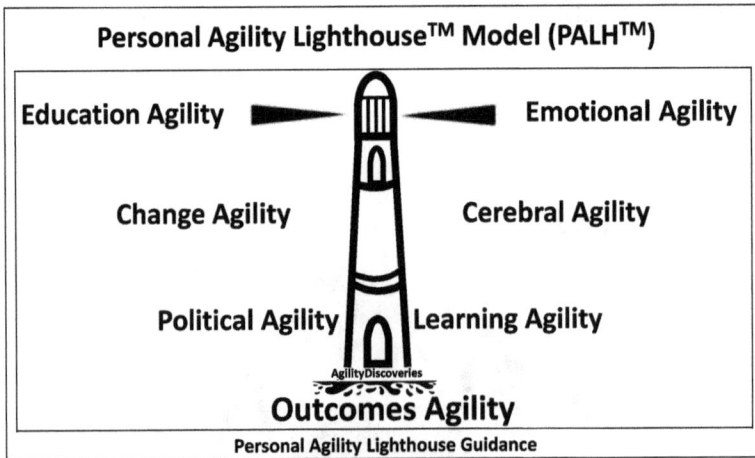

Personal Agility Lighthouse™ Model (PALH™)

Education Agility ► ◄ Emotional Agility

Change Agility   Cerebral Agility

Political Agility   Learning Agility

AgilityDiscoveries

Outcomes Agility

Personal Agility Lighthouse Guidance

Raji Sivaraman & Michal Raczka 2017

Personal Agility is the future competency for Organizational Agility transformation.

People with highly honed Personal Agility can create enhanced Organizational Agility.

APPENDIX—PALH™ SELF-ANALYSIS INDEX

Self-Analysis from Personal Agility to Organizational Agility is a tool that can be used to check your Personal Agility Lighthouse (PALH™) Index. You can check if and how the seven flavors are in balance and which of the seven flavors of our PALH™ model are honed and which of them can be improved.

We as authors of the book and founders of AgilityDicoveries.com are happy to share the Personal Agility Lighthouse Index. Below you can find the current version of the self-analysis. But please keep in mind that the PALH™ Index is constantly improving according to our current and continuous research and findings. If you want to check your personal scores, please contact us via our website (http://agilitydiscoveries.com/) and we will be very happy to send you the newest version. When you score yourself and send the results to us, we will provide you a report with the overall scores and interpretation. However, we request that it is important for you to let us know your feedback about the book and the self-analysis because that will enable us to create a new lighthouse for you for your space. Looking forward to receiving your scores and helping you all to reach your ogled lighthouse!!

Self-Analysis from Personal Agility to Organizational Agility

Please read the statements below carefully and circle them based on how the listed statements reflect to you on any given working day. No points should be given more than once for one statement. Please score points as given below:

- 100% Me = 5 points
- In most cases it is Me = 4 points
- Neither here nor there = 3 points
- In most cases not Me = 2 points
- Not Me at all = 1 point

Statement No		Points				
1	I always act on Last Responsible Moment mode	1	2	3	4	5
2	I always align process and people	1	2	3	4	5
3	I am always a team player	1	2	3	4	5
4	I am always brave to accept the fact that we can be wrong about our assumptions	1	2	3	4	5
5	I am always comfortable making decisions between options	1	2	3	4	5
6	I am always entrepreneurial and initiative minded	1	2	3	4	5
7	I am always flexible in problem-solving	1	2	3	4	5
8	I am always fluent in dealing with stakeholders' wants	1	2	3	4	5
9	I always aim to inspire others	1	2	3	4	5
10	I am never afraid of change	1	2	3	4	5
11	I am always looking beyond what I know already	1	2	3	4	5
12	I am always open to new discoveries	1	2	3	4	5
13	I am always pushing to excel beyond my limit	1	2	3	4	5
14	I am always transparent	1	2	3	4	5
15	I always analyze business decisions before I implement them	1	2	3	4	5
16	I always try to give guidance to others	1	2	3	4	5
17	I always communicate what my vision is	1	2	3	4	5
18	I always communicate what the team vision is	1	2	3	4	5
19	I always deal with different considerations of others	1	2	3	4	5
20	I always cope with different requirements of others	1	2	3	4	5
21	I always feel other's difficulties	1	2	3	4	5
22	I always bring new viewpoints	1	2	3	4	5
23	I always have the courage to admit that I do not know everything	1	2	3	4	5
24	I always kill skepticism	1	2	3	4	5
25	I always like to know more, read more, be curious	1	2	3	4	5
26	I always like to put myself in another's shoes	1	2	3	4	5
27	I always seek clarity	1	2	3	4	5
28	I always show ease in difficult and obscure situations	1	2	3	4	5
29	I always strive for excellence	1	2	3	4	5
30	I always take charge of my moods, thoughts, behaviors	1	2	3	4	5
31	I am always adaptable	1	2	3	4	5
32	I always think of many options when it comes to politics	1	2	3	4	5
33	I always tolerate challenging situations	1	2	3	4	5
34	I always understand my own moods, thoughts, behaviors	1	2	3	4	5
35	I always understand others' moods, thoughts, behaviors	1	2	3	4	5

Notes

Introduction

1. Scaled Agile. n.d. "Enterprise Challenges." https://www.scaledagile.com/enterprise-solutions/enterprise-challenges/, (accessed June 9, 2020).
2. Balticpmconference.eu. 2017. "Project Management Development—Practice and Perspectives." http://www.balticpmconference.eu/sites/default/files/image-uploads/proceeding_book_26.04.2017_final.pdf, (accessed August 2, 2018).
3. Ijmas.iraj.in. 2016. "IJMAS—Volume-2, Issue-9, Special Issue-1 (Sep 2016)." http://ijmas.iraj.in/volume.php?volume_id=300, (accessed August 2, 2018).
4. Psychology.fas.harvard.edu. 2007. "David McClelland." https://psychology.fas.harvard.edu/people/david-mcclelland, (accessed August 2, 2018).
5. Managementstudyguide.com. 2018. "Expectancy Theory of Motivation." https://www.managementstudyguide.com/expectancy-theory-motivation.htm, (accessed August 2, 2018).
6. Wikipedia. n.d. "Ideation (Creative Process)." https://en.wikipedia.org/wiki/Ideation_(creative_process), (accessed June 9, 2020).

Chapter 1

1. C. Wilson, R. Sivaraman. 2016. *Making Projects Sing: A Musical Perspective of Project Management* (New York: Business Expert Press).
2. Pmi.org. 2018. "PMI's Pulse of the Profession In-Depth Report: Navigating Complexity." https://www.pmi.org/-/media/pmi/documents/public/pdf/learning/thought-leadership/pulse/navigating-complexity.pdf, (accessed August 2, 2018).
3. Pmi.org. 2018. "The Triple Constraint." https://www.pmi.org/learning/library/triple-constraint-erroneous-useless-value-8024, (accessed August 2, 2018).
4. Netpromotersystem.com. 2018. "Bain & Company: Net Promoter System—Processes." http://www.netpromotersystem.com/system-processes/index.aspx, accessed August 2, 2018).
5. Forbes.com. 2018. "Ten Leadership Lies 90% of Managers Believe." https://www.forbes.com/sites/lizryan/2018/03/31/ten-leadership-lies-90-of-managers-believe/#771e5fd86b67, (accessed August 2, 2018).

6. Pmi.org. 2014. "Do Your Projects Fail?". https://www.pmi.org/learning/library/system-of-work-influences-project-management-9868 (accessed August 2, 2018).

7. World Economic Forum. 2016. "This Skill Could Save Your Job—And Your Company." https://www.weforum.org/agenda/2016/08/this-little-known-skill-will-save-your-job-and-your-company/, (accessed August 2, 2018).

8. T. Chamorro-Premuzic, M. Swan. 2016. "It's the Company's Job to Help Employees Learn." https://hbr.org/2016/07/its-the-companys-job-to-help-employees-learn, (accessed May 29, 2020).

Chapter 2

1. N. Grover. 2019. "31 Ellen DeGeneres Quotes to Make Your Day Awesome." https://positivelifeproject.com/31-ellen-degeneres-quotes-to-make-your-day-awesome/, (accessed June 15, 2020).

2. D.E. Weeks. 2016. "The DevOps Equation: Agility + Empathy = Quality." https://devops.com/devops-equation-agility-empathy-quality/, (accessed June 15, 2020).

3. R. Goldberg. n.d. "Run User Experiments to Validate Your Hypothesis." https://www.ibm.com/garage/method/practices/think/practice_run_user_experiments/, (accessed June 15, 2020).

4. Wikipedia. n.d. "T-shaped Skills." https://en.wikipedia.org/wiki/T-shaped_skills, (accessed June 15, 2020).

5. R.F. Dam, Y.S. Teo. 2020. "Personas—A Simple Introduction." https://www.interaction-design.org/literature/article/personas-why-and-how-you-should-use-them, (accessed June 15, 2020).

6. Scrumstudy.com. 2014. "*Collaboration in Scrum* Project." https://www.scrumstudy.com/whyscrum/scrum-collaboration, (accessed August 3, 2018).

7. Elcompanies.com. 2018. "Learning & Development." https://www.elcompanies.com/talent/working-here/learning-and-development, (accessed August 3, 2018).

Chapter 3

1. "Sandra E. Peterson Quotes." https://www.brainyquote.com/authors/sandra_e_peterson, (accessed June 9, 2020).

2. Ambysoft.com. 2018. "Examining the Agile Manifesto." http://www.ambysoft.com/essays/agileManifesto.html, (accessed August 2, 2018).

3. Optimizely, n.d. "A/B Testing." https://www.optimizely.com/optimization-glossary/ab-testing/, (accessed June 9, 2020).

4. E. Kim. 2017. "Amazon Just Launched a New Training Program to Help Employees in Danger of Being Fired," *Business Insider*. https://www .businessinsider.com/amazon-launches-pivot-program-help-employees-in-danger-of-being-fired-2017-1, (accessed August 2, 2018).

5. ProductPlan, n.d. "Kano Model." https://www.productplan.com/glossary/ kano-model/, (accessed June 9, 2020).

Chapter 4

1. ACADOCEO, n.d. "22 Inspirational Quotes from Apple CEO Tim Cook." http://acadoceo.com/22-inspirational-quotes-from-apple-ceo-tim-cook/, (accessed June 9, 2020).

2. J. Vara. 2014. "Individuals and Interactions over Processes and Tools," *Scrumandkanban.co.uk*. https://scrumandkanban.co.uk/individuals-and-inter-actions-over-processes-and-tools/, (accessed August 3, 2018).

3. J. Shelly. 2015. "Hey Urban Outfitters, Stop Treating Like They Won the Cool-Job Lottery," *Philadelphia Magazine*. https://www.phillymag.com/ business/2015/10/12/urban-outfitters-employees/, (accessed August 3, 2018).

Chapter 5

1. Goodreads. https://www.goodreads.com/quotes/6707427-when-something-is-important-enough-you-do-it-even-if, (accessed June 9, 2020).

2. M. Berteig. 2015. "The Agile Manifesto—Essay 2: Individuals and Interactions over Processes and Tools—Agile Advice," *Agile Advice*. http://www.agileadvice .com/2015/01/13/agilemanagement/the-agile-manifesto-essay-2-individuals-and-interactions-over-processes-and-tool, (accessed August 3, 2018).

3. Medium. 2016. "The Agile Supply Chain Management: What is it and why should you care!" https://medium.com/supply-chain-hubspot/the-agile-supply-chain-management-what-is-it-and-why-should-you-care-966ad9829d19, (accessed August 3, 2018).

4. R. Knight. 2017. "How to Work with Someone Who's Always Stressed Out," Harvard Business Review. https://hbr.org/2017/08/how-to-work-with-someone-whos-always-stressed-out, (accessed June 9, 2020).

Chapter 6

1. AZ Quotes. https://www.azquotes.com/quote/922185, (accessed June 9, 2020).

2. B. de Langhe, S. Puntoni, R. Larrick. 2017. "Linear Thinking in a Nonlinear World." https://hbr.org/2017/05/linear-thinking-in-a-nonlinear-world, (accessed June 9, 2020).

3. S. Denning. 2017. "Julian Birkinshaw's Fast/Forward: How Agile Builds Action-Oriented Firms," *Forbes.com*. https://www.forbes.com/sites/stevedenning/2017/06/24/julian-birkinshaws-fastforward-how-agile-builds-action-oriented-firms/#2c37cb861406, (accessed June 9, 2020).

4. P. McCord. 2014. "How Netflix Reinvented HR." *Harvard Business Review*. https://hbr.org/2014/01/how-netflix-reinvented-hr, (accessed August 3, 2018).

Chapter 7

1. A. Meah. n.d. "35 Inspirational Satya Nadella Quotes on Success." https://awakenthegreatnesswithin.com/35-inspirational-satya-nadella-quotes-on-success/, (accessed June 12, 2020).

2. Agile Forest. 2012. "Working Software over Comprehensive Documentation." https://agileforest.com/2012/11/30/working-software-over-comprehensive-documentation/, (accessed August 3, 2018).

3. GV. n.d. "The Design Sprint." https://www.gv.com/sprint/, (accessed June 12, 2020)

4. Forbes.com. 2017. "How To Speed Up Your Computer With These 7 Solutions." https://www.forbes.com/sites/forbes-finds/2018/08/03/how-to-speed-up-your-computer-with-these-7-solutions/#3de6b39d5b11, (accessed August 3, 2018).

5. Amazon Jobs. n.d. "Leadership Principles." https://www.amazon.jobs/en/principles, (accessed June 12, 2020).

Chapter 8

1. GeckoandFly. 2020. "32 Jack Ma Quotes on Entrepreneurship, Success, Failure and Competition." https://www.geckoandfly.com/20175/jack-ma-quotes/, (accessed June 12, 2020).

2. Amazon. https://www.amazon.com/Habits-Highly-Effective-People-Powerful/dp/0743269519, (accessed June 12, 2020).

3. D. Mills-Scofield. 2012. "It's Not Just Semantics: Managing Outcomes vs. Outputs." https://hbr.org/2012/11/its-not-just-semantics-managing-outcomes, (accessed June 12, 2020).

4. H. van der Pol. 2018. "Outcomes vs Outputs: Are You Activity or Results Driven?" https://www.perdoo.com/resources/outcomes-vs-outputs/, (accessed June 12, 2020).

5. S. Denning. 2011. "Measuring What Matters: from Outputs to Outcomes: Part 2." https://www.forbes.com/sites/stevedenning/2011/02/27/measuring-what-matters-from-outputs-to-outcomes-part-2/, (accessed June 12, 2020).

6. D.G. Amen, D. Highum, R. Licata, J.A. Annibali, L. Somner, H.E. Pigott, D.V. Taylor, M. Trujillo, A. Newberg, T. Henderson, K. Willeumier. 2012. "Specific Ways Brain SPECT Imaging Enhances Clinical Psychiatric Practice," *Journal of Psychoactive Drugs* 44, no. 2, pp. 96–106. Tandfonline.com. (2012). https://www.tandfonline.com/doi/abs/10.1080/02791072.2012.6 84615, (accessed August 3, 2018).

7. Brightline. https://www.brightline.org/, (accessed June 12, 2020).

8. S. Noben. 2019. "The Quarterly Business Review." https://www.linkedin.com/ pulse/quarterly-business-review-sonja-noben/?articleId=6608269228141223936, (accessed June 12, 2020).

9. Management 3.0. n.d. "OKRs (Objective and Key Results)." https:// management30.com/practice/okrs/, (accessed June 12, 2020).

10. Agile Manifesto. n.d. "Principles behind the Agile Manifesto." https:// agilemanifesto.org/principles.html, (accessed June 12, 2020).

11. M. Drill. 2019. "Agile: Continuous improvement through Retrospectives." https://medium.com/swlh/agile-continuous-improvement-through-retrospectives-3df7095bc6a1, (accessed June 12, 2020).

Chapter 9

1. T. Woodall. 2015. "QOD-086: Jim Rohn—Discipline Is the Bridge between Goals and Accomplishments." http://www.goalgettingpodcast .com/qod-086-jim-rohn-discipline-is-the-bridge-between-goals-and-accomplishments/, (accessed June 12, 2020).

2. The Business Professor. n.d. "Pareto Analysis—Definition." https:// thebusinessprofessor.com/knowledge-base/pareto-analysis-definition/, (accessed June 12, 2020).

3. J. Whitehurst. 2015. "Managing Performance When It's Hard to Measure." https://hbr.org/2015/05/managing-performance-when-its-hard-to-measure, (accessed June 12, 2020).

4. State of Agile. n.d. "State of Agile Report." https://www.stateofagile .com/#ufh-c-473508-state-of-agile-report, (accessed June 12, 2020).

5. W. Aghina, C. Handscomb, J. Ludolph, D. West, A. Yip. 2018. "How to Select and Develop Individuals for Successful Agile Teams: A Practical Guide." https://www.mckinsey.com/business-functions/organization/our-insights/how-to-select-and-develop-individuals-for-successful-agile-teams-a-practical-guide, (accessed June 12, 2020).

6. Shen-Nong. n.d. "What Is the Yin Yang Theory?" www.shen-nong.com/ eng/principles/whatyinyang.html, (accessed June 12, 2020).

7. Scrum.org. n.d. "What Is Scrum?" https://www.scrum.org/resources/what-is-scrum, (accessed June 12, 2020).

Chapter 10

1. AZQuotes.com. n.d. "Bill Gates." https://www.azquotes.com/quote/843556, (accessed May 13, 2019).
2. L. Richards. 2008. "NASA Technical Reports Server (NTRS)," *Reference Reviews* 22, no. 8, pp. 40–41.
3. Pmi.org. 2012. "Organizational Agility." https://www.pmi.org/-/media/pmi/documents/public/pdf/white-papers/org-agility-where-speed-meets-strategy.pdf, (accessed August 5, 2018).
4. M.C. Layton. "Applying Agile Management Value 1: Individuals and Interactions Over Processes and Tools." https://www.dummies.com/careers/project-management/applying-agile-management-value-1-individuals-and-interactions-over-processes-and-tools/, (accessed June 12, 2020).
5. G. Wagenaar, S. Overbeek, G. Lucassen, S. Brinkkemper, K. Schneider. 2018. "Working Software Over Comprehensive Documentation—Rationales of Agile Teams for Artefacts Usage." *Journal of Software Engineering Research and Development* 6, Article 7. doi:10.1186/s40411-018-0051-7.
6. K. Molokken-Ostvold, K. M. Furulund. 2007. "The Relationship between Customer Collaboration and Software Project Overruns," *Agile 2007*, Washington, DC, 2007, pp. 72–83. doi: 10.1109/AGILE.2007.57.
7. C. Williams, D. Kessler. 2013. "Agile Manifesto—Responding to Change over Following a Plan." https://www.sourceallies.com/2013/08/agile-manifesto-responding-to-change-over-following-a-plan/, (accessed June 12, 2020).
8. Strefapmi.pl. 2018. "Kwartalnik Project Management Institute Poland Chapter." https://strefapmi.pl/wp-content/uploads/2018/06/Strefa-PMI-21.2018.pdf, (accessed August 3, 2018).
9. W.S. Rahula. n.d. "The Noble Eightfold Path." https://tricycle.org/magazine/noble-eightfold-path/, (accessed June 12, 2020).

Chapter 11

1. A. Meah. n.d. "20 Inspirational Larry Ellison Quotes on Success." https://www.awakenthegreatnesswithin.com/20-inspirational-larry-ellison-quotes-on-success/, (accessed June 12, 2020).
2. Wikipedia. n.d. "Intelligence." https://en.wikipedia.org/wiki/Intelligence, (accessed June 12, 2020).
3. McKinsey & Company. 2017. "Going from Fragile to Agile." http://www.mckinsey.com/business-functions/organization/our-insights/going-from-fragile-to-agile, (accessed June 12, 2020).

Suggested Further Reading

Agility Discoveries. http://agilitydiscoveries.com/, (accessed June 12, 2020).

Agility Discoveries. n.d. "Articles—Personal Agility for Organizational Agility using our PALH™ Model." http://agilitydiscoveries.com/articles/, (accessed June 12, 2020).

Project Design Management. 2018. "Revista," pp. 66–71. http://project designmanagement.com.br/produto/revista-79/, (accessed June 12, 2020).

P. Emīls. 2017. "Report on the Sixth International Scientific Conference on Project Management in the Baltic Countries. Project Management Development—Practice and Perspectives." *PM World Journal*, VI, no. V. https://pmworldlibrary.net/wp-content/uploads/2017/05/pmwj58-May2017-Pulmanis-Latvia-conference-report.pdf, (accessed June 12, 2020).

R. Sivaraman and M. Raczka. June 2017. "A Project Manager's Personal Agility Sightings." *PM World Journal*, VI, no. VI. https://pmworldlibrary.net/article/a-project-managers-personal-agility-sightings/, (accessed June 12, 2020).

R. Sivaraman and M. Raczka. February 2018. Cruise from Personal Agility to Organizational Agility. *PM World Journal*, VII, no. II. https://pmworldlibrary.net/wp-content/uploads/2018/02/pmwj67-Feb2018-Raji-Sivaraman-Michal-Raczka-Cruise-from-Personal-Agility-to-Organizational-Agility.pdf, (accessed June 12, 2020).

Sixth International Scientific Conference on Project Management in the Baltic Countries. "Project Management Development—Practice and Perspectives," Riga, Latvia, April 27–28, 2017, p. 268. http://www.balticpmconference.eu/sites/default/files/image-uploads/proceeding_book_26.04.2017_final.pdf, (accessed June 12, 2020).

Sixth International Scientific Conference on Project Management in the Baltic Countries. "Project Management Development—Practice and Perspectives," Riga, Latvia, April 27–28, 2017. http://balticpmconference

.eu/sites/default/files/image-uploads/proceeding_book_26.04.2017_
final.pdf, (accessed June 12, 2020).

Strefapmi.pl. 2018. "Kwartalnik Project Management Institute Poland
Chapter," p.6.https://strefapmi.pl/wp-content/uploads/2018/06/Strefa-
PMI-21.2018.pdf, (accessed June 12, 2020).

Note

All Industry applications can be found in depth at:
https://www.iris.xyz/contributor/raji-and-michal.

About the Authors

Raji Sivaraman, **MS, PMI-ACP, PMP, PMO-CP Principal of ASBA LLC,** a Singapore citizen, helps USA/Singapore companies with strategic planning/overseas start-ups. Speaks several languages. Worked in Singapore, Thailand, India, and the USA. Facilitates Fortune 50/500 companies with CSR/BSR/ Mobility projects. Consultant, Director, Strategic Advisor, and an Advisory Board member for nonprofit/for-profit organizations. Worked in IT, publishing, financial, standards, and logistics industries. Adjunct Professor at Montclair University, USA. Researcher, Author, Contributor to Project Management books, published articles, research and white papers internationally. Global facilitator, keynote speaker, Discussant/Academic chair, panelist, Moderator for CXO Forum. An Agile practitioner, a Pracademic. **Distinguished Women leaders of Singapore, 2013**.

Cofounder of AgilityDiscoveries (http://agilitydiscoveries.com)
LinkedIn: https://www.linkedin.com/in/raji-sivaraman-m-s-pmi-acp-pmp-pmo-cp-01b12613/

Michal Raczka, **MBA, PMI-ACP, PMP, PSPO, AgilePM, CISA,** a Polish citizen, a project management expert, experienced in new technologies and digital leadership fields. Currently, he is the IT Director at mBank S.A. He is also a project management lecturer at executive MBA programs. He has conducted several organizational changes involving the optimization of project management methods and agile transformations. Always keeps Team in the center. Value and results focused with lean and agile approach. Individual with proven achievements in project management, business management, process improvement, and team leadership. Experienced in managing geographically distributed, multidisciplinary projects and customer teams. Experienced in project excellence awards assessments. Conference speaker. Strategic Advisor. Lecturer. Volunteer. Mentor.

Cofounder of AgilityDiscoveries (http://agilitydiscoveries.com)
LinkedIn: https://linkedin.com/in/mraczka

Index

OTHER TITLES IN OUR PORTFOLIO AND PROJECT MANAGEMENT COLLECTION

Timothy Kloppenborg, *Editor*

- *Project Communications: A Critical Factor for Project Success* by Connie Plowman and Jill Diffendal
- *Quantitative Tools of Project Management* by David L. Olson
- *The People Project Triangle: Balancing Delivery, Business-as-Usual, and People's Welfare* by Stuart Copeland and Andy Coaton
- *How to Fail at Change Management: A Manager's Guide to the Pitfalls of Managing Change* by James Marion and John Lewis
- *Core Concepts of Project Management* by David L. Olson
- *Projects, Programs, and Portfolios in Strategic Organizational Transformation* by James Jiang and Gary Klein
- *Capital Project Management, Volume III: Evolutionary Forces* by Robert N. McGrath
- *Capital Project Management, Volume II: Capital Project Finance* by Robert N. McGrath
- *Capital Project Management, Volume I: Capital Project Strategy* by Robert N. McGrath
- *Executing Global Projects: A Practical Guide to Applying the PMBOK Framework in the Global Environment* by James Marion and Tracey Richardson
- *Project Communication from Start to Finish: The Dynamics of Organizational Success* by Geraldine E. Hynes
- *The Lost Art of Planning Projects* by Louise Worsley and Christopher Worsley
- *Project Portfolio Management, Second Edition: A Model for Improved Decision Making* by Clive N. Enoch
- *Adaptive Project Planning* by Louise Worsley and Christopher Worsley
- *Passion, Persistence, and Patience: Key Skills for Achieving Project Success* by Alfonso Bucero
- *Leveraging Business Analysis for Project Success, Second Edition* by Vicki James
- *Project Management Essentials, Second Edition* by Kathryn N. Wells and Timothy J. Kloppenborg
- *Agile Working and the Digital Workspace: Best Practices for Designing and Implementing Productivity* by John Eary

Announcing the Business Expert Press Digital Library

Concise e-books business students need for classroom and research

This book can also be purchased in an e-book collection by your library as

- *a one-time purchase,*
- *that is owned forever,*
- *allows for simultaneous readers,*
- *has no restrictions on printing, and*
- *can be downloaded as PDFs from within the library community.*

Our digital library collections are a great solution to beat the rising cost of textbooks. E-books can be loaded into their course management systems or onto students' e-book readers.
The **Business Expert Press** digital libraries are very affordable, with no obligation to buy in future years. For more information, please visit **www.businessexpertpress.com/librarians**.
To set up a trial in the United States, please email **sales@businessexpertpress.com**.

www.ingramcontent.com/pod-product-compliance
Lightning Source LLC
Chambersburg PA
CBHW061328220326
41599CB00026B/5085